Damn the Nanny...

This is EXTREME Parenting!

S. Kelley Chambers

TotalRecall Publications, Inc.

TotalRecall Publications, Inc..
1103 Middlecreek
Friendswood, Texas 77546
1-281-992-3131
www.totalrecallpress.com

All rights reserved. Except as permitted under the United States Copyright Act of 1976, No part of this publication may be reproduced, stored in a retrieval system, or transmitted in any form or by any means electronic or mechanical or by photocopying, recording, or otherwise without prior permission of the publisher. Exclusive worldwide content publication / distribution by TotalRecall Publications, Inc.

Copyright © 2015 by: S. Kelley Chambers

ISBN: 978-1-59095-198-9
UPC 6-43977-41980-4

Printed in the United States of America with simultaneously printings in Australia, Canada, and United Kingdom.
FIRST EDITION
1 2 3 4 5 6 7 8 9 10

Judgments as to the suitability of the information herein is the purchaser's responsibility. TotalRecall Publications, Inc. extends no warranties, makes no representations, and assumes no responsibility as to the accuracy or suitability of such information for application to the purchaser's intended purposes or for consequences of its use except as described herein.

The scanning, uploading and distribution of this book via the Internet or via any other means without the permission of the publisher is illegal and punishable by law. Please purchase only authorized electronic editions, and do not participate in or encourage electronic piracy of copyrighted materials. Your support of the author's rights is appreciated.

To my children:
LaCrystal C. Smith,
Quasim W. Chambers,
Travonte S. Montivero, and
Desmond J. Weinberg-Jones

Acknowledgments

Without the grace, love, and mercy of the Lord, I would have lost my mind a long time ago, so I thank God above all others for my sanity and peace. I would especially like to thank my husband, Darrin E. Chambers for supporting my ideas and visions and for standing beside me through it all, even when it seemed difficult. Thank you for your unselfish labor and patience. To family members that supported me from the very beginning; my mother, Mary C. Smith and my mother in-law, Barbara F. Chambers. To my sisters who gave me, wisdom encouragement and support; Wandra Wells, S. Angel Jameson-Jones, Tammy Rodriquez, and Rowena Venable, Mona Lisa Tatum, Regina Wright, Deanna Ellison and Brenda Benson, thank you for the bonds formed through the struggles over the years. To my one brother, Eric Smith Sr. To my sister-friends; Bernadette Tyler, Catherine Bowman, Dionne Little, Glenda Driggers, Yvonne Taylor, Vernita Burrell, and Tara Ouden, you believed in me at ground zero and your support has meant the world to me, thank you for faithfully trusting in my dreams. To Tracy Price of Dazzles for being a dynamic stylist, your hands hold a gift. To my close friends; Khadijah Henderson, Reymonte Washington, Yvette Smith, Evongline Tinsley, and Bruce Boyd, you believed in me and I am grateful for your friendship. To my mentor: Bishop Mary Adams, thank you for your honesty and prayers. To my youngest protégé; Lundon Lynch, keep writing sweetie. To Victoria Jackson-Wallace, even though we've drifted apart, you are always in my heart.

To the Riverside Writers BAM Monday night Critique Group, thank you so much for performing critique surgery on my manuscript. To Anna Hill, my first editor, thank you for helping me and enjoying every bit of the correction process. To my final editor, Sigrid Macdonald, I am grateful to you for your sharp eye, expertise and understanding. You're the greatest.

Donna and Larry Turner, you opened up unimaginable opportunities for me. You lit a fire and there is no hose strong enough to put it out. God bless you. To John Wills, thank you for seeing a special gift in my words and willingly becoming my unpaid agent/mentor. I pray you have much success with your books. To Bruce Moran of Total Recall Publishing Inc., you took a chance and stepped out on faith. Bless you.

A List of Characters

Character name: Kelley Chambers (Mom, Ma, Mommy)
Mother of four, protagonist and back-bone of the family and of this book. She is very out-spoken and honest, and holds character, respect for authority and personal accountability in high esteem. Unfortunately, those principals do not go over too well with her teenagers.

Character name: Darrin Chambers (Dad)
Father of four, a passive and extremely non-confrontational workaholic. He uses work as an emotional escape, but every so often intervenes and shows an enormous amount of strength and character.

Character name: LaCrystal
The oldest of four children, LaCrystal is very reserved, has an outgoing and fun personality, but wants to fit in with peers so badly, she is willing to compromises her convictions, but quickly learns that the best thing to be in this world, is to be yourself.

Character name: Quasim
The oldest male of three boys, he has a very strong personality and all the traits of a gifted leader. Unfortunately, Quasim's defiance, disrespect and aversion to authority causes him numerous problems as he tries to sort through his choices and learn from the outcomes.

Character name: Travonté
The middle child and peacemaker, Travonté is filled with compassion and laughter. As he grows into a young man, he seeks approval from others and ultimately it becomes his undoing.

Character name: Desmond

The youngest of the family. Desmond is quiet, reserved and intelligent. He stands strong in his convictions and would rather think independently and be unaccepted than fall victim to peer pressure.

Introduction

    Sitting knee to knee on hard wooden benches, I warily scanned the solemn faces of parents and relatives around the room. Mothers nervously rubbed tightly clasped hands buried in their laps, others shoulders heaved up and down as they silently cried into balled-up crumpled tissues. Fathers dressed in starched shirts and print ties leaned against the walls with their arms crossed and eyes distant. Disruptive teenagers brazenly laughed and joked with familiar faces across the crowded courtroom waiting area.

    Various races and economic backgrounds all brought together by one common factor: our children. Each of us anxiously waited for his or her child's name to be called to stand in front of the judge. Each of us waited to hear our child's fate in this ongoing nondiscriminatory fight to save our children from their own destructive behaviors.

    Have you ever looked at your rebellious teenager and wondered, "Who is this person?" or cried yourself to sleep, only to wake in the middle of the night pondering, "Where did I go wrong?" We did. Raising children can be a rewarding experience, but when the teen becomes extremely defiant, disrespectful, and abusive, the challenge can be exhausting and nearly impossible.

    There are no secrets or guidelines to nurturing perfect kids. Moreover, if you are looking for a tutorial that outlines methods to raising Stepford-like children, this is not it. Besides, if you have ever imagined taking your child back to a store to apologize for stealing; made him or her go to school dressed-up as a punishment for disrespecting the teacher, or volunteered to chaperone an unsupervised teen party, because all of the popular kids were going to be there and if your child did not attend they would just die, then you may appreciate some of the corrective methods used in this book.

    Our four children; LaCrystal, Quasim, Travonté, and Desmond, each present his or her own unpredictable and occasionally explosive confrontations in this memorable collection of stories. As parents, my husband, Darrin, and I acknowledge we made some mistakes. We also learned to pray and forgive, and many more valuable lessons along the journey from elementary through high school.

Read on to find out how extreme creative disciplinary methods were used to teach our children responsibility and accountability for their actions through unconventional tough-love.

Table of Contents

Acknowledgments IV
A List of Characters... VI
Introduction VIII

I. Elementary School: Don't Start No #@*~, Won't Be No #@*~   XII

Chapter 1 Money like Oprah 1
Chapter 2 SS Video Game 4
Chapter 3 Barbershop 101 7
Chapter 4 Camel Spit 12
Chapter 5 All You Can Eat Buffet 17
Chapter 6 Video Game De-Programming................................20
Chapter 7 An Old Fashioned Christmas 23
Chapter 8 Alice Doesn't Live Here! 28
Chapter 9 Potty Mouth Antidote...33
Chapter 10 A Can of Whup-Az' 38
Chapter 11 Lunch Bully 46
Chapter 12 Picasso's Understudy..50
Chapter 13 Roll the Dice 53
Chapter 14 A Series of Unfortunate Pets.................................60
Chapter 15 Bubble Bath Dilemma 67

II. Middle School: You Better Act like You Know   72

Chapter 16 Vigilante Feline..73
Chapter 17 Copacabana 77
Chapter 18 Spiderman 83
Chapter 19 Sock Trolls 88
Chapter 20 Suit Boy..91
Chapter 21 Plumbing 101 96
Chapter 22 Target Practice 99

Chapter 23 Lip-Popping.. 104
Chapter 24 Next Stop-the Olympics.. 106
Chapter 25 Batman... 112
Chapter 26 Saved by *"The Pursuit of Happyness"* 115

III. High School: 'You Don't Know Squat About Life At Sixteen' 117

Chapter 27 Mom: The New Anti-theft Device 118
Chapter 28 A Halloween Memory... 129
Chapter 29 "The roof, the roof, the roof is on fire" 137
Chapter 30 Do Your Pants Hang Low?... 140
Chapter 31 My Name Ain't Clara Belle 150
Chapter 32 Free Tutoring... 154
Chapter 33 Boomerang Phone.. 160
Chapter 34 Las Vegas Slots... 164
Chapter 35 Earthquake... 171
Chapter 36 A Political View.. 183
Chapter 37 Shopping Cart Lifting 189
Epilogue... 194

I.
Elementary School: Don't Start No #@*~, Won't Be No #@*~

Chapter 1
Money like Oprah

"It's not fair!" ten-year-old Desmond screamed as he stomped down the stairs to clean up the mess he made in his bedroom.

"I hate this house!" He screamed at the top of his lungs while stomping back and forth around the basement.

"Good," I yelled as I leaned over the handrail, "I hate messes, so now we are even!"

My husband, Darrin and I, noticed that as each of our children hit the age of ten, they began to make personal demands while denying parental requests. When Desmond reached fifth grade, like the others before him, he felt as if he had some type of royalty privileges.

The kitchen sits directly above the bedroom our three boys; Quasim, Travonté and Desmond share. Our daughter, LaCrystal's bedroom is upstairs with ours. On this particular Saturday morning, I was in the kitchen preparing Patti LaBelle's homemade buttermilk biscuits, so I could hear Desmond throwing shoes and other heavy articles against the bedroom door and hitting the walls. I turned up the volume on the radio, hoping the music would drown out his temper tantrum. Even though he is the youngest in the family, his defiance reigned supreme. He forcefully opened the bedroom door and yelled upstairs at me.

"It's not fair! I hate this house and I hate you!"

I turned down the music, walked over to the stairs and looked over the banister.

"Life isn't fair! Deal with it! If life was fair, then I would have a face like Halle Berry, a body like Beyoncé, and money like Oprah Winfrey. But since I am stuck with what God gave me, so are you."

He slammed the bedroom door and continued yelling that he hated me.

I shouted over the railing at the closed door, "Save all of your hate words for the Christmas season. Remind me that you hate me and you don't want me spending hundreds of dollars on you. But for now, get that room cleaned because inspection is in one hour."

The month of December is the most peaceful month of the year. You would think our children were walking around strumming harps and singing angelic hymns. Darrin and I have absolutely no trouble the entire month. The trash is taken out without a fuss; they bathe without an argument, clean their bedrooms and even volunteer to clean the kitchen. After the toys and games are broken, lost or the novelty wears off, they mutate back into ungrateful spawns who talk-back and behave disrespectfully. Well, I was fed-up with their selfishness and bad attitudes.

The bedroom door swung open again and Desmond angrily yelled upstairs, "One hour! I can't clean all of this mess up in one hour! It took me a whole week to make this mess."

"Well then," I calmly stated, "you better stop throwing stuff and start cleaning up and when you're done, a plate will be in the oven, but you won't eat until I inspect."

"Shit!" He screamed and began growling and mumbling under his breath. He slammed the door and started throwing stuff against the walls again. I made a mental note of his potty-mouth, but decided to deal with one problem at a time. I finished making a big breakfast of hot; butter-milk biscuits, sizzling bacon drizzled with maple syrup, and oatmeal seasoned with brown sugar, plump raisins, pecans, and cinnamon. I made sure I left the oven on low so the aromas of the foods wafted through the air.

He called me downstairs an hour later and I inspected his side of the bedroom. The shoes were neatly placed under the bed. The clothes were placed in dirty clothes hampers, the bed was made and disheveled papers were placed neatly on his dresser. It was clean! I thanked him for a job well done and reminded him that his plate was waiting for him in the oven as I went back upstairs to the kitchen. When he came upstairs to eat he apologized for his behavior. I told him I appreciated the apology and reminded him that we could not afford a live-in maid, so until I received a genie in a magic lamp with three wishes or money like Oprah, anyone who made a mess would have to clean it up.

Chapter 2
SS Video Game

Quasim loved his new hand-held Game Boy Advance. He played it regularly, at the breakfast table, during lunch, and at dinner. He played it while watching TV, doing his homework, and occasionally, while he was falling asleep. A few times I had to pry it out of his fingers while he slept. When he was told to put the game away, he would hide it for a few minutes until he thought no one was looking, then he would pull it out and start playing it again.

Darrin and I limited Quasim's playing time to weekends by taking the game away on Sunday nights prior to bedtime. We placed it on a bookshelf in our bedroom and locked our bedroom door during the weekdays while we were at work. On Saturday mornings, we would give him the Game Boy for the weekend.

One particular Saturday, I went to retrieve the Game Boy and found that it was no longer on the bookshelf where I had placed it. It was sitting on top of the TV. The following week, I placed it on the dresser but it ended up on the bookshelf. Finally, I placed the Game Boy in our bathroom in a cabinet drawer, when I went to retrieve it on Saturday it was back on the bookshelf. To make matters worse, we received a letter from Quasim's school telling us that Quasim's homework was not being turned in and his grades were dropping.

I knew I had to prepare a punishment that would address violating our privacy and cause him to focus on his academics. I decided to patiently wait and watch for two weeks before I acted.

One evening during dinner, Darrin and I broached the subject and asked Quasim about his homework. We wanted to know why he felt his grades were declining. He shrugged his shoulders and nonchalantly told us that he forgot to turn in his homework.

I asked in a voice as calmly as I could muster, "You're at school for 7 hours and you forget to turn in your homework? Are you in class or are you on a space shuttle orbiting Earth while everyone else is in school?"

"I just forget," he casually stated. "I don't see why it's such a big deal anyway."

"Do you forget to go to breakfast and lunch?" Darrin asked. Without answering, and with a dumbfounded look on his face, Quasim started looking around the dining room.

"Did you know that since you don't have excellent grades and your test scores are average, when you do the homework you receive points that are added to your letter grade and they can actually help improve your chances of passing?" Darrin explained to him.

Rolling his eyes, Quasim replied, "Yes, I know how the grading system works," insinuating he was fed up with our questioning. "I'm not worried about that, I'll get my grades up before the grading period ends." He blatantly informed us. He finished dinner, completed his homework and without a second thought went to watch TV until bedtime. His two-week time period was coming very close to ending and my patience was running low.

After several calls and a few meetings with his teacher's, we agreed upon them sending home a homework completion form on Friday's. When he was assigned homework; he completed it, the teacher initialed it, and on Fridays a form with each teacher's signature was sent home confirming his progress.

This worked for a week until Quasim brought home excuses: He had a substitute teacher, there was no homework, the teacher walked out of class and never returned, and the class was in the library all day. He faithfully came upstairs every Saturday pleading for the Game Boy though.

One Saturday afternoon he came upstairs begging to get his Game Boy and I handed it to him. He smiled, took it, and went downstairs. I went downstairs a few minutes later and found him sprawled out on the dining room floor and his fingers were moving so fast across the buttons on the Game Boy they looked mechanical. It was time to put my plan in action so I casually strolled over to him and I asked for the video game. He slowly sat up and handed it to me, silently watching as I pulled the cartridge out. I went into the bathroom, lifted the toilet seat lid, and dropped the cartridge into the toilet. Plop! It floated down to the bottom and settled in a corner.

He ran into the bathroom after me, pushing me out of the way and looked into the toilet. His mouth opened and closed like a guppy. I dropped the entire Game Boy into the toilet. It drifted to the bottom and rested beside the cartridge.

"Are you crazy?" He shouted.

"No," I calmly stated. "But if you think we will allow you to continue breaking into our bedroom every week in search of that Game Boy, playing it all day and lying about your school work, then you are crazy."

"This is crazy, I can't believe you!" He continued to shout as he angrily paced around the toilet like a predator circling prey.

"You better believe it, buddy. I will be as crazy as the Mad Hatter before I allow you to continue with this addictive behavior." I turned and walked out of the bathroom just as he reached into the toilet to retrieve the game pieces.

Later, I learned he tried to dry the game pieces, but it never worked the same. Eventually, his homework started coming home, it was completed and turned in on time, and surely enough the grades improved.

Chapter 3
Barbershop 101

I was sitting at my desk reading on my break when I received a call from the sixth grade principal.

"Mrs. Chambers, are you sitting down?"

"Yes," I replied as I closed the book. "I am."

"Desmond is being suspended for three days. Apparently, during art class he took out a pair of scissors and clipped off a classmate's pony-tail."

"You're kidding me, right?"

"We're sending home a disciplinary referral, for a three-day suspension, but it's up to the parents of the other student if they plan to press criminal charges. The staff and I are looking into expelling him, but we have agreed to wait until you discipline him. We like your form of discipline, and it seems to work better than anything we can give students."

I was definitely going to put Desmond back into therapy until graduation. Instead of going to the senior prom, he would be sitting in a therapist's chair dressed in a cummerbund and tuxedo.

"Hello, Mrs. Chambers, are you still there?"

"Yes, I am here."

"We'd like to give you a few days to think of a suitable punishment at home because the school is unsure of which disciplinary action to take for this particular situation. Do you have any idea of how you plan to handle this?"

I told him I had no idea at the time, but I would contact him later during the week. I called Darrin and told him of the incident. After the initial shock, he asked me what "I" planned to do about Desmond. Why was everyone pushing the discipline on me? I did not have all the answers. Was the staff afraid to discipline a sixth-grader?

I left work early and got home a few minutes before the school buses dropped off the students. Desmond arrived home and saw me sitting at the dining room table. He slid into a chair next to me. I remained completely silent. Several minutes passed before he attempted to explain his version of the incident.

After repeatedly insisting the girl was his friend and that she gave him permission to cut her hair, he informed me that her parents would be okay with the cut. After all, he only cut off a little bit. The principal was exaggerating.

"Son, do you know that you can be criminally charged? Furthermore, do you even understand what criminally charged means?"

A blank stare confirmed he had no clue as to the gravity of his actions. He truly believed it was a minor incident that was blown out of proportion.

Darrin came home, looked at Desmond, shook his head, and without a word, went upstairs to take a shower. Shortly afterwards, LaCrystal and Quasim arrived home from high school. They cautiously surveyed the situation and shook their heads before going to start their homework. I continued talking to Desmond.

"What in the world was going through your head, Desmond? I don't have the time or patience to be sitting in court or the principal's office over such senseless and reckless behavior. If you have uncontrollable thoughts running through your head, please, let me know so I can try to seek professional help for you."

"There is nothing running through my head."

"I figured that. But why did you do it?"

"I was bored."

"You were bored? Lord, give me strength."

I got up and walked a few steps away, making sure I was more than an arm's distance away from him. I looked out the window at the trees and took a couple of deep breaths.

"I send books, scribble pads, pens—and weren't you in art class today? Did drawing something ever cross your mind? You don't just sit in class and cut somebody's hair because you're bored. If you want to take cosmetology class, wait until high school!"

Travonté arrived home. He and Desmond attended the same school. Before going downstairs he told Desmond that the other kids were talking about him. Desmond lowered his head.

"Stupid!" Travonté yelled and ran downstairs.

"I wanted to cut her hair and she let me! What's it to you anyway?" Desmond blurted out.

"You have lost your mind! You are trying your best to make me go there. Don't move, I'll be right back!"

I ran upstairs to get my cosmetic mirror; a comb, a towel and hair-clippers. He continued to sit at the table. After neatly placing the items on the kitchen counter, I called Desmond over.

"Son, come sit on the bar stool. Since you like to cut hair, I would like to see your skills, and you can start on your own head."

"I don't want my hair cut. I just wanted to see if I could cut her hair. Anyway, she asked me to cut her hair because she's my friend."

I patted the barstool two times. He took two large steps back, pressing his back against the kitchen sink, and distancing himself from me. His hands were balled into tight fists; I noticed his biceps flexing as his breathing became deep and sporadic and his face a deep shade of red.

"Why do we have to do this?" he screamed.

"Son, I am going to say this as calmly as I can. Please don't take my quietness as a weakness. It is in your best interest to release your fists because if you hit me, I promise you, I will light a fire under your ass so intense it will take fire departments from two counties to put it out."

He gradually relaxed, unclenched his fists, approached the stool, sat down, and took the clippers from my hand. Our other children were silently crowding into the kitchen. I leaned against the counter.

"All of you can do better than this. I don't want any of you to grow up and blame your misfortunes on the world, your race, the system, or your parents. You have a choice; either play the victim or make something out of your life."

I looked into each of their eyes while nodding my head slightly, acknowledging each of them. There was relief on their faces because they were not the ones receiving the punishment, but they all understood the lesson to be learned. As I spoke, Desmond was still holding the clippers and looking at the floor. I could hear him humming a faint tune, which was his way of mentally drowning out my voice.

I walked over, took his hand and turned on the clippers. It started buzzing and vibrating. He dropped it to the floor, jumped up, threw his head back and ran around the kitchen in circles wailing loudly, "I don't want my hair cut! I don't want my hair cut! It's not fair! You can't do this!"

Darrin came downstairs and stood in the kitchen's entrance. Desmond stopped and looked at him.

"Her parents did not ask you to cut her hair, did they?" He asked Desmond. "Did they send a letter to school giving you the authority to style their daughter's hair?"

"No."

"Furthermore, show me your cosmetology license."

"I don't know how to cut hair!" he bawled.

"That didn't stop you in class, did it? Do unto others as you would have them do unto you."

I picked up the clippers, called him over to the stool, and proceeded to cut his hair. It went well until the guard kept getting tangled in his hair and slipping off, leaving a bald spot. When I was done, he resembled a well-loved, but tattered, teddy-bear.

Later that night, Desmond came upstairs to our bedroom and told us that he was going to write an apology letter to his classmate, her parents, and one to the principal. We agreed that his decision was a wonderful idea, and if he needed any help, we would assist him. The next day, I located a good therapist and I never had to open "the barbershop" again.

Chapter 4
Camel Spit

One spring day I received a call from Desmond's fifth-grade teacher. She complained that Desmond and two other students used notebook paper and paper-towels to make spitballs and proceeded to throw and then spit them at other children. They were sent to the principal's office and were being put on a one-day suspension. She then took a deep breath and told me that I would have to come in and meet with the principal before Desmond would be allowed back in school.

I had no more annual or sick leave on my job. Taking another day off for my kid's behavior issue was beginning to jeopardize my position.

I hung up the phone. I was beginning to sweat and my thoughts were a mess. What was he thinking? My concentration was completely gone as I left work and took an early train home.

Going upstairs to our bathroom, I claimed a few minutes of quiet time before approaching Desmond. I sat on the toilet and began to pray for patience, tolerance and a sound mind. I knew my anger at this point could escalate and become out-of-control. I had to stay in control to teach him how his behavior could affect his education and his relationship with his peers.

After deeply meditating and I was sure my emotions were stable, I knew what had to be done. I went downstairs with four Q-tips in my hands. I called Desmond into the kitchen and asked him to swab the inside of his mouth.

"Why? Why do you need my spit on Q-tips?" He asked as he took two from my hand and placed them in his mouth.

"I have to send it to a forensics lab to have it tested."

"Why do you need to test it?"

"Because that is the only way I will know if your DNA is a direct link to Jesus Christ or one of His Disciples."

He looked at me with a puzzled expression.

"Huh?" he asked and shrugged his shoulders. "What do you mean?"

"You must have lost your cotton-picking mind? Are you a camel, because camel's spit? And if you think I will tolerate you spitting on people, you'd better think twice, buddy! The only reason why you should feel your spit is appropriate to touch anyone's skin, is if it's Divine or ordained by God Himself! While you're running around acting like a caveman did you stop to think of how you would feel if someone hit you with a spitball?"

He quietly stood in the kitchen looking at me then looking around as if I was the one losing my mind.

"If I was still a kid and you threw spitballs and hit me, I would've grabbed you, knocked you silly and then chased you home while kicking the dust out of your pants."

He explained how he and some friends thought it would be fun to spitball the bathroom ceiling. When they got bored, they began throwing spitballs on students. He tried to excuse his behavior by saying he and his friends didn't actually hurt anyone, the wads of toilet paper were just wet and they stuck.

I did not have the patience to hear any more of his excuses because they only meant that he had not learned a lesson from being suspended. I sent him to his room.

He went to work with me on the day of his suspension. I refused to let him stay home watching TV, drinking up the kool-aid and tea, and eating all of the cereal and snacks in the house.

He sat in my office chair, completed all missed assignments, practiced cursive handwriting, and completed spelling and language worksheets I found on the Internet. I had every intention of keeping him busy.

The morning of the school meeting, I called him into the kitchen and handed him a roll of paper-towels. On the counter was a cup of water and a plastic pail.

"What do you expect me to do with these?" he asked as he looked down at the items on the counter and then at me.

"Bless your sweet little heart," I cooed. "You don't have a clue, do you? Let me explain: I expect you to make spitballs like the ones you made at school, fill the pail with all of your spitballs, then we will go to the meeting, and you can pass out your spitballs to anyone wanting to hold one."

His eyes fixed coldly on the pail and paper-towels. I could tell he was contemplating if he should act out defiantly or adhere to the discipline.

"Make it snappy." I said as I turned and went upstairs to doodle around and kill time, giving him ample time to comprehend the motive and lesson in all of this.

After several minutes had passed, I came down the stairs and found him sitting in the kitchen on a stool. He was ripping the paper-towels into small strips, and placing each strip into his mouth. Slowly chewing, he slid long wet strips of paper-towel from his mouth, leaving a trail of spittle hanging from his lower lip and dropped each one into the pail.

"Son is that what a spitball looks like or is it supposed to be balled up? I want them to look just like the ones you made in school. You do remember how you made them, don't you? You do remember how much fun it was to make them, don't you?"

He began furiously ripping paper-towels, balling them up in his hands, popping them into his mouth, chewing for a few seconds and then throwing them into the pail.

Several minutes later he was moving much slower as

dryness in his mouth caused him to realize the whole idea was not as much fun as he expected. I went upstairs and brought down a large neon green poster board that I purchased earlier during the year for school projects. I sat down in the kitchen beside him on a stool and wrote on the poster board in big bold letters:

FREE SPITBALLS
GERMS MIXED WITH
YESTERDAY'S LUNCH

Desmond peeked over to see what I was writing. After reading the sign he shouted, "I'm sorry, I won't do it again. This is too embarrassing. You're crazy. I won't do it. I won't wear the sign. You always go to the extreme with punishments. Whatever happened to getting a belt and beating your kid? Why do you have to do weird stuff all the time to teach us a lesson? I won't wear it!"

"Oh son," I calmly replied, "you will wear it or we won't go to the meeting, and that means you will not be allowed back in school to cause trouble and then you'll get sent to an alternative school and you'll repeat the fifth grade."

He gave me what I call the *Firestarter* look. His eyes were so piercing that if he had fire-like mutant powers, he would have lit me up like a Roman candle on the Fourth of July. Instead, out of respect, humility and a change-of-heart miracle, he allowed me to pin the poster board to the front of his dress shirt and tie.

I had called the principal earlier that morning and told him of the plan to have Desmond sit in the front office with the pail and sign while I was in the meeting. He agreed. I had no intention of actually allowing him to pass out those gross spitballs, but I was not about to let him know that.

We entered the school and sat in the front office. Desmond's classmates immediately came up to him to read the sign. They looked in the pail and snickered behind their hands while whispering to each other. I glanced at him a couple of times as we waited for the principal to call us. He kept his head down. I felt sympathetic, but I refused to give-in and have him believe this type of behavior was acceptable, funny, or would ever be tolerated again.

I met with the principal first. We discussed how I was handling the situation at home and he told me that if it happened again, they would look into expelling him. Desmond was called into the office next and he was chastised by the principal. Surprisingly, he lowered his head and apologized with complete sincerity. I walked over to him, took the poster board and pail from him, and asked him if he thought he should apologize to his teachers and classmates. He agreed.

As we walked down the long corridor together, he kept his head down. We entered his classroom and he went directly to the front of the class and got everyone's attention. He told them that he was ashamed of his behavior and that it would never happen again. He explained to everyone that he did not expect his mother to carry the punishment to such extremes and had he known she was going to get "stupid" he would have thought twice. He then turned to me and apologized for putting me in such an embarrassing position because of his behavior.

I choked up for a few seconds as I walked over and pulled him to me. I hugged him tightly and thanked him for accepting responsibility for his actions. We smiled at each other as I kissed him on his forehead before leaving. He never threw another spitball...

Chapter 5
All You Can Eat Buffet

Darrin would not pour himself a glass of iced tea even if the air conditioner broke on a sweltering summer day. On this particular work-day, the three-hour commute from Fredericksburg to Washington, DC, which is usually an hour and a half ride, left us irritable, exhausted and famished.

We were running late, so I called home and instructed Quasim, our oldest son, step-by-step directions on warming up a meal I prepared the previous day. Sitting in the refrigerator was a green bean casserole seasoned with a dash of garlic, black pepper, sliced Yukon Gold potatoes, cream of mushroom soup, an onion, and turkey wings. There was also a tray of uncooked chicken strips, a Ziploc-bag filled with seasoning, and a pot of steamed rice.

I instructed Quasim, who was in fifth grade at the time, to turn the oven to 300 degrees and place the casserole and the pot of rice in the oven. I told him I would fry the chicken when I arrived home. Quasim begged me to allow him to cook the chicken strips, but, I refused. I was not comfortable with him frying foods or cooking with hot oils when no adult was around to supervise. He argued otherwise, insisting that I needed to let him grow up and stop treating him like a baby. After all, he was almost in middle school, he thoughtfully reminded me. I reluctantly agreed and told him that he was welcome to heat the dinner for everyone, but if any problems arose, he was to call me immediately.

When Darrin and I finally made it home; he went upstairs to shower while I placed my purse on the kitchen counter, walked over to the sink, and washed my hands, all the while glancing around and seeing empty pots and pans. I turned and looked at Quasim's grease smeared face.

"Son, do not tell me that you ate an entire tray of chicken strips, a whole casserole, and the pot of rice? That was a family meal."

"Yup," he smiled, "I was hungry and I'm a growing boy." He let out a loud burp and gloated.

I looked at him long and hard. Indeed, he was growing taller and slimmer and it was a joy to see him enjoy my cooking, but I was not about to watch my growing young man sit smugly at the table, stuffed and content, while everyone else wondered what was for dinner, and I was not about to eat Corn Pops.

"Quasim, since that meal was for a family and you ate the entire thing, I expect you have a plan for the family to eat dinner, since I am too tired to start over again."

"No," he stated. "You can just make something else."

"No son, I cannot. But you will. I am going upstairs to shower. Please start dinner." I said as I walked upstairs to the bathroom.

"And by the way, I don't eat Ramen Noodles or Oodles N' Noodles."

"I can't make a whole dinner by myself," he reluctantly pleaded.

"Oh yes you can," I replied, "and you will, so grab a cookbook, Pillsbury Doughboy, and get started."

He started ranting and raving about how it wasn't fair and he didn't care what I said, he wasn't cooking a whole dinner. To stop myself from going back downstairs, grabbing a plastic spatula and beating him senseless, I started humming a tune as I showered and attempted to block out the sounds as kitchen cabinet doors were being violently slammed.

I took an additional long time in the bathroom and claimed it as my "Peace of Mind" time.

I prayed to the Lord for the strength to make it through the night without slapping that child silly. I relaxed and went downstairs. Quasim placed a bag of frozen Whiting fish on the kitchen counter along with some flour as I entered. I whispered a silent thankful prayer for his attempt, because if I had not seen the effort I probably would have grabbed the spatula and then this book would have never been completed because I would be in jail.

I put the flour back and replaced it with fish seasoning. He stood behind me, watching my every move. I told him to soak the fish in cold water and he did as directed.

While he was doing that, I took out some large white potatoes, rinsed them, cut a slit in them, and placed them in the microwave. I told him to cut the fish pieces in half and then roll them in seasoning while I poured vegetable oil into a frying pan. I insisted he fry the fish while I placed a pot of sweet corn-niblets on the stove. When dinner was finished, while everyone else was eating, I thanked him for the dinner and poured him a large cup of prune juice.

"What is this?" he asked.

"Oh, you are going to get that dinner out of you one way or another," I explained. He looked completely perplexed.

"Furthermore, all of that food will stop you up and give you heartburn and indigestion problems."

"Do I have to drink it all?"

"Yup," I smugly replied.

Later that night, after everyone had gone to bed, Quasim came and asked me for a few extra rolls of toilet-paper.

Chapter 6
Video Game De-Programming

Darrin listened quietly as I told him about Quasim playing the PlayStation game system every morning before school, immediately after school, and once I was awakened at one o'clock in the morning only to find him playing video games.

"I believe it has become another game addiction."

"Then I will bring the entire system upstairs, and he will only be allowed to play it on the weekend," Darrin replied. "We've had to do this once before with that hand-held video game."

Eventually, we placed the PlayStation in our bedroom. After a few weeks, I began noticing changes. Each time I went to place a music CD in the PlayStation, I had to remove a Madden football DVD. One Monday morning, before leaving for work, I intentionally left a Disney DVD in the PlayStation and checked it daily to see when it was removed. By Friday night it was replaced with a Madden DVD.

Quasim was breaking into our bedroom to play video games. It was time for him to pay the piper and Saturday night would fit my plans perfectly.

Late Saturday night around eleven o'clock, I called Quasim into our bedroom and gave him permission to play PlayStation "all night." A large smile, showing almost every tooth in his mouth, spread across his face. His eyes began dancing back-and-forth as he looked from the TV to me, to the game-system and then back to me. He could not believe his luck, or so he thought. To him this was the ultimate privilege. His wishes had finally come true. He had had hit the ultimate jack-pot.

"You can play all night, but it has to be in my presence."

"Whatever!" He joyfully exclaimed hopping from foot-to-foot. "Just give me the controller!"

He sat down in front of the TV, put in the Madden game, grabbed the PlayStation's controller, humped his back and began intensely playing the video game. Within minutes his eyes were glossed over and everything not affiliated with the game became obsolete, as his hands rapidly moved over the buttons.

Darrin and I climbed into bed. I dozed lightly, all the while listening to him as he sat on the floor at the foot of our bed in Video Heaven (or Hell depending on your point of view). After three hours Quasim grew tired. I heard him attempting to get up and turn off the PlayStation. I jolted up.

"Oh no son, you have the PlayStation all night!"

"But I'm tired and I don't want to play anymore."

"But you must play I was just starting to get the hang of the game by watching you."

He sat back down and I forced my eyes to stay open for an additional hour as he played with little enthusiasm. The novelty and excitement was definitely waning. I drifted off to sleep for a few minutes. When I opened my eyes he had fallen asleep with the controller in his hands and his head rested on the foot of our bed. I got out of bed, walked over to him and shook his shoulder repeatedly. I started badgering him with questions.

"What level are we on now? Huh? Huh? What level?"

"What are you talking about?" He sleepily growled. "I'm tired and don't want to play anymore."

Quasim knows that our bedroom is off limits unless it is an emergency, but since our rules were broken repeatedly for this game, I insisted we keep playing. I was going to make sure we would never have this problem again. I got back into bed as he continued to play. Darrin slept through it all.

After a few minutes, Quasim's head was nodding and bobbing again. I slowly crawled to the foot of the bed, lightly shook his shoulder, and crawled back under the covers. He played for a few more minutes then began to slightly nod again. It was time to put my fail proof plan into action.

This time I crawled to the foot of the bed, made sure he was sound asleep, then got close to his ear and loudly whispered in his ear with as much enthusiasm as I could muster, "Quasim, show me which player is yours? Which team member are you, gray or blue? Can I change my team colors to hot pink? I like hot pink. What about teal-green or purple? Do you think they have teal-green and purple colors? Can we start over so I can change my team jersey colors? Do they have cheerleaders? Huh, Quasim, do you think they have cheerleaders? Can I dress the cheerleaders? Can I fix their hair? Can we start the game over?"

Just hearing my voice irritated him so much it brought tears to his eyes. He probably would have jumped off the balcony to get away from my annoying voice at this point.

"Okay, Okay!" He yelled. "I know what you're doing. The gig is up. I was sneaking in your room to play the game and I'm sorry. Okay. I'm sorry. It won't happen again."

"Are you sure? I can keep this up until sunrise if you feel it's worth violating the rules. We set rules for a reason, when you choose to break them it is our job to help you understand the consequences for your actions."

"I'm really sorry," he said and started crying. I got off the bed, hugged him close and told him that I accepted his apology. I reminded him that we expected him to live up to his part of the weekend only video game agreement. He agreed and stuck to his word.

Chapter 7
An Old Fashioned Christmas

A few weeks before Christmas, I thought it would be a good idea if our family experienced an old fashioned, homemade holiday bonding project. The *Good Housekeeping* clay ornament instruction that I ripped out of a magazine while at the doctor's office was beginning to look quite easy.

One cold December, Saturday afternoon, I called everyone away from the TV and told them of my idea to save money by making our own ornaments. Chatting excitedly, they took a seat at the dining room table. I placed wax paper in front of them and proceeded to mix a white paste consisting of flour, salt, and water in a large wooden bowl. After everyone got a chance to stir, I separated the mixture, giving each of them a large amount.

We made a wonderful mess, straying completely away from the step-by-step instructions and not caring one bit. Food coloring was added to some mixtures, vanilla or cinnamon flavors were added to others, giving it a home-baked smell and every so often, Quasim licked his clay, made a weird face and exclaimed, "Eww, this tastes like salt."

I'm guessing each time he licked the concoction he expected it to have a different taste because he kept doing it. I reminded everyone to make holes for string so we would be able to hang the ornaments on the tree, but Quasim paid no attention as he shaped and snuck licks.

The next morning we got up early, hurried downstairs in

our pajamas and began to paint the ornaments, which dried rather quickly, so we were able to string and hang a few of them on the tree. Quasim looked up with wide eyes and exclaimed, "Hey, mine has no holes. How will I hang them?"

"I told you to make holes while you were eating the clay, Einstein."

"But I didn't hear you."

After a few minutes, he grabbed a fork and attempted to poke a hole in the hardened ornament. Crack! It split in half.

"I think I pressed too hard."

He reached for another ornament and started twisting and pushing the tip of the fork into it. Crack! Within a few minutes he was sitting at the table looking dumbfounded, with a pile of cracked, painted salt-flour clay pieces in front of him.

When the project was completed, we all took a good look at our ornaments sitting on the table, and hanging on the tree, and came to the conclusion that they were horrendous. We trashed them, ate breakfast, showered, and went to church.

After dinner, I pulled one of my cookbooks out of the cabinet. I still felt energetic, and ready to start another Christmas project. The idea of making gingerbread men with real ingredients sounded fascinating. I tuned the radio to 97.1, the Christmas music station during the holidays, and called everyone into the kitchen again. They were given new instructions.

We immediately started working on a mixture. Each person peeked in the book then ran to add the next ingredient, sometimes adding the same ingredient twice, while bumping into each other, spilling flour, sugar and molasses on the countertops and floors.

"Wow! That's going to make a whole lot of gingerbread men." LaCrystal exclaimed as she peered into the large bowl. Then without measuring, she dumped in extra baking powder.

"Smells good," Quasim exclaimed excitedly, as he closed his

eyes, lifted his chin, and sniffed the air. They kept stirring, smiling, singing to the Christmas music playing on the kitchen radio, laughing, and adding ingredients.

"Mom," LaCrystal whispered as she stopped in the center of the kitchen and looked at the rising dough, "I think this is way too much mix."

She walked over to the cookbook, picked it up, read it, and gasped. "Mom, this recipe was for a serving of fifty people. Didn't you read it? What are we going to do with all of this mix? If we eat it, our farts will smell like gingerbread for the rest of the year."

"We'll eat it! We'll eat it!" Quasim chanted as he rolled and popped a chunk of dough into his mouth and hopped from one foot to the other.

"We'll make gingerbread men, eat some, hang a few on the tree and freeze the rest." I told them.

"Until when," LaCrystal shrieked, "The Resurrection? I'm not eating gingerbread every day!"

"I'll eat it! I'll eat it!" A grinning, drooling Quasim repeatedly chimed.

The mixture continued to rise and was beginning to overflow the edges of the large bowl so we rolled it out and placed piles of dough onto wax paper. Each person used a different six-inch cookie cutter for gingerbread men, stars, bells, stockings and anything else we could think of that would embrace the Christmas season and use up the dough. LaCrystal decided she wanted to make something different and added the impression of skirts and hair before officially ordaining hers as gingerbread divas.

To hang some of the cookie ornaments on the tree, we poked holes in the top and placed them in the oven, then began cleaning up the mess. All remaining dough was wrapped and placed in the freezer for future projects. I went into the dining room to clear the table while everyone else worked in the kitchen.

"Mom, I think you should come and see this." Quasim yelled from the kitchen.

"What is it?"

"Just come and see."

I walked into the kitchen and peered through the glass oven window. The gingerbread men and women had risen to three or four inches and were steadily rising. They were connecting to each other like string dolls and had lost the original shape.

LaCrystal came and peered at her gingerbread divas. They were puffed up to four inches also, but only in the abdominal area.

"Eww! Gross! They're pregnant. I don't want them. I don't want pregnant gingerbread women."

"I'll eat them!" Quasim readily volunteered. I allowed them to eat the over-stuffed gingerbread men and women as we stood in the kitchen looking clueless and thinking of what we could attempt to make next.

LaCrystal stared at me for a long while before asking me if I could make anything in the arts and crafts department because everything I had tried so far sucked. I took the insult a little painfully, but pretended not to hear her. I sat on a kitchen stool, defeated. This just wasn't turning out the way I envisioned. I was running out of options, ingredients, and confidence.

Suddenly, I remembered a scene from the classic show, *Little House on the Prairie*. The family did not have any money for expensive Christmas gifts, so they made their own. I had sheets of felt material in various colors left over from numerous failed projects, stored in a supply bin.

I ran upstairs to my container and pulled out all the brown, beige, and black felt material that my arms could carry. I grabbed glue-guns, scissors, glue sticks, yarn, stuffing, mini stick-on eyeballs, and pipe cleaners. I was determined that one of us was going to make at least one successful ornament that weekend.

Again, we sat down at the dining room table, with a little less enthusiasm but with lots of concentration and determination, and attempted to cut out little body patterns. We used the glue gun to seal the edges of the crooked gingerbread men then filled them with stuffing. We glued on eyes and small beads for buttons. LaCrystal used additional yarn to glue hair and necklaces on some of hers. She was determined to hang fashionable ornaments and I was determined to hang all our monstrosities on the tree that year. We had a very blessed and Merry Christmas!

Chapter 8

Alice Doesn't Live Here!

Every week something was broken or turned up missing in our home. We were tired of patching holes in walls, replacing TV's, appliances, dishes, and bedroom doors. I stood in the kitchen one dreary summer afternoon looking at a drawer that was hanging off the hinges. What next I wondered.

My thoughts were interrupted when Quasim came bounding up the stairs.

"Mom, Desmond just threw the TV remote and broke it and I'm tired of him intentionally breaking stuff whenever he gets angry. Can I have my own TV in my room?"

"Sure, as soon as you are in a dorm or your own apartment, you may have whatever size TV you want if you pay for it." He looked at me for a moment, rolled his eyes, then turned around and headed down the stairs.

"Desmond, please come upstairs. Now!"

He entered the kitchen, plopped down on a bar stool and looked down at the tile. I folded my arms and leaned against the dishwasher. I patiently gave him a few minutes to get his thoughts together.

"I am waiting to hear your explanation of what happened downstairs."

"I still had two minutes of my TV time and Quasim changed the channel."

"So the way to let him know your TV time was not up, was by making sure no one else would be able to watch TV?"

"I didn't want him to watch TV for taking two minutes of my time so I broke it. There, are you satisfied?"

"Do I detect an attitude? I am sure you know that you just broke the remote that I purchased, and I would appreciate it if you would lower the bass in your voice. You don't do wrong and become pompous when confronted."

I was determined he would take full responsibility for his actions. Damn the nanny, there was no *Alice* from *The Brady Bunch* running around cleaning up after my kids and taking the blame for their mistakes, this was his mess and he would deal with it.

Our children are required to read for half an hour every day and write a report at the end of each chapter then they are paid an allowance at the end of each book. I knew Desmond was saving up for an expensive skateboard, but this was his mess, he would have to clean it up.

"I tell you what, go downstairs and get your allowance for the books you've read, hop your cocky-little butt on your bicycle and go to the store and purchase another TV remote."

He jumped up and pointed out the window. "Can't you see that it's starting to drizzle outside? I don't know where to buy a stupid remote anyway."

"You should have thought about the weather when you decided to act like *The Hulk* and started breaking things. Furthermore, unless you can show me a stable in Bethlehem where you were born, you better stop acting like you deserve preferential treatment. If you do something wrong, accept the consequences."

I turned my back to him and continued investigating the damage to the kitchen drawer. I refused to entertain a back-and-forth discussion about it.

"I'm not going out in the rain and I don't care what you say!" He yelled at my back.

"I don't know why you are worrying about that light drizzle

it might do you some good."

"Why isn't Quasim in trouble for stealing my two minutes?"

I peered over my shoulder. "You could have come and told me, but you didn't. That was your choice. I don't care what transpired downstairs while you were watching TV. No one has the right to break the remote that I purchased. So you're getting out of here and you're not coming back without a remote, and a receipt showing you paid for it."

He stood in the kitchen breathing hard, growling deeply under his breath, and giving me that old familiar *Firestarter* look.

"You can either ride your bicycle up to the Rite Aid Pharmacy and Dollar General Store or you can ride in the county sheriff car. Take your pick!"

"Arrgh, I hate you!"

"Whatever! Save that drama for Christmas."

I tuned my radio and began humming to drown out his tantrum. He slammed the door as he was putting on his jacket and leaving out to get his bike. I peered out the window to check the weather. It was still lightly drizzling, and the sky was cloudy, but nothing to get into a panic over. At least that is what I thought.

For some reason, it was as if the clouds were waiting to punish him because a few minutes after he left, the sky darkened, loud claps of thunder and lightning ripped across the sky, then suddenly the clouds released a monsoon. The rains were so heavy I was unable to see the cars in the parking lot a few feet away as I peeked out the window. I panicked and bolted upstairs, all the while praying Desmond did not get struck by lightning.

"Darrin," I shouted, "I sent Desmond to the store and I need you to go out and find him!" He was lying across the bed watching TV. He sprang up when a loud crack of thunder ripped through the sky.

"Where did you send him?" He asked while putting on his shoes. I followed behind him as he grabbed his keys and went downstairs toward the front door.

"I sent him to Rite Aid and the Dollar General Store. He couldn't have gone too far, he left a few minutes ago and he's on his bicycle."

Darrin ran out in the rain to the car, only to return an hour later tired, drenched and without Desmond. I snatched the dish towel off the counter and opened the front door for him. He ran directly in from the car, shielding his eyes with his hands. I handed him the towel.

"I didn't see him anywhere. I drove the route to the pharmacy and the Dollar General and I went in both stores, walked up-and-down each aisle, questioned the cashiers and then drove the route again before coming back here. I didn't see him anywhere." He handed the towel back to me. "He'll be alright. He has sense enough to seek shelter. I'm going to take a shower because I am tired, wet and hungry."

"You're right. He probably found shelter until the storm stops." I nervously stated, mostly reassuring myself. I decided to wait around in the kitchen until Desmond returned. I tried not to think the worst as I peeked out the window every so often. Since the glue was not working, I placed the broken drawer on the counter and made a mental note to add it to Darrin's "House-hold Fix-it" list and began preparing ingredients to make banana pudding.

While standing at the counter slicing bananas into a deep-dish glass baking pan, with my back to the entrance, I began to feel an overwhelming negative presence, like someone was squeezing me from behind. Goose-pimples rose on my arms, and I slowly turned.

I screamed and jumped backwards. A shadowy, menacing figure stood in the foyer. It took me seconds to recognize Desmond. If he had been wearing a long trench coat, I would have wasted a tray of banana pudding on him. He was drenched from head- to-toe. Water dripped from his thick, dark eyebrows and eyelashes. The rain had parted his hair down the middle and it hung in heavy wet clumps, dropping water onto the floor. His wet clothing hung loosely off his body, forming large puddles around him. His face was contorted with sheer rage.

I pressed my backside against the cabinet. If the rain had made him crazy and he tried to charge me, I was going to take him down like a Gladiator in a coliseum battle, pudding pan and all.

"Here is your stupid-freaking remote!" He slammed the remote on the counter with such force I thought he would break that one too. He headed downstairs to change out of the wet clothes.

I regained my composure and finished the banana pudding. Come to think of it, every since I required everyone to replace what they broke, with their own money, things are breaking less and less frequently.

Chapter 9
Potty Mouth Antidote

For weeks, Desmond had been screaming profanity at anyone or anything that upset him. I took him to several specialists and he received a battery of tests. The findings showed no emotional, mental, chemical or physical imbalances that would cause violent or verbal outbursts.

I was beginning to think he liked hearing curse words. If he was told to clean up after himself, he would start shouting, "I hate this shit!" and "Fuck it, I'm not doing it!"

The weekly punishments were not effective, so during this period, I stayed more than an arms distance away to avoid hitting him and knocking him into another galaxy. He did not know it but every night I was on my knees praying to God for patience, direction and restraint.

For an entire month I made Desmond look up every profane word he used in various dictionaries. If he found it, he was to write the definition and then look in the Thesaurus and locate a word to replace it. That calmed his fiery tongue for a few days, but within two weeks, he was back to fluctuating between a hardcore rap artist and a drunken sailor.

Saturday is our weekly clean-up day. The boys rotate their chores and on this particular morning, the bathroom was being cleaned by Travonté, the family room by Quasim, and the bedroom by Desmond.

I was in the kitchen preparing maple bacon, oatmeal, and homemade buttermilk biscuits for breakfast when I overheard Travonté politely ask Desmond to come into the bathroom and get his dirty clothes off the floor. I walked over to the railing leading to the basement and listened as Desmond stomped into the bathroom, picked up his clothes, stomped out and slammed the door behind himself while screaming at the top of his lungs, "Fuck you!"

Travonté ran up the stairs to find me and tell on Desmond, but when he saw me leaning over the railing listening, he stopped, acknowledged my presence and went back downstairs to finish cleaning the bathroom.

Leaving the bacon frying, I went upstairs to LaCrystal's bedroom and pulled her karaoke machine down from a top shelf in her closet. I wiped it off and took it down to the kitchen.

I got index cards and a marker out of a drawer and proceeded to write down all the profanity I remembered Desmond saying over the previous weeks, as well as things I was told he said in the last few months. I placed the index cards on the kitchen counter, the karaoke machine on the dining room table and called everyone to breakfast.

As breakfast was ending, we quietly sat at the dining room table. I was sure everyone had had a good look at the karaoke machine and was wondering why it was sitting on the table. I got up and slowly carried it into the living room. Everyone turned and watched me as I plugged it in and started testing it, making an intentional scene.

"Testing one-two. Testing, testing." I loudly spoke into the microphone over and over. They looked at each other, shrugging their shoulders, waiting in anticipation. When I was sure the suspense was driving them mad, I placed the microphone on the hook and went back to my plate. I quietly sat down and sipped my cup of tea.

Each of them waited for confirmation that someone might know what was about to take place.

"Are we about to have another family talent show?" Quasim finally blurted out. We had a home-made show a few months earlier and everyone got a chance to display a talent. We all voted on the winner and Quasim won by a unanimous decision with a rap song by Tupac.

I remained silent. As they got up to wash their plates, I approached Desmond as he was about to go downstairs. I put my hands on his shoulders and gently stopped him.

"Son, I set up the karaoke machine for you."

"Huh?"

Everyone stopped what they were doing and looked at me with wide eyes, as if I were a popping and locking monkey in a pink polka-dot tutu.

"Desmond, you will recite your profanity and hate words every 15 minutes with 5 minute intervals for an hour. You are allowed to shout every cuss word that you know or that you can think of. I want you to get it all out of your system because personally, I am sick and tired of hearing you cussing people out for no reason. It stops here, today!"

He looked at me with a sly grin, as if he was about to outsmart me, pulled away and went into the living room. He stood over the karaoke machine, looked at it for a few seconds and was about to pick up the microphone when I said in a sing-song voice, "Oh no son, you must plug it outside. You will be rotating inside for thirty minutes and outside for thirty minutes."

The sly grin quickly turned into a frown. His eyes searched my face in desperation. "Do I have to stand outside on the deck cursing?"

"Yes, you do."

"But people will think I'm crazy."

"That didn't stop you from changing that potty mouth before, did it?"

"No," he said with his head bowed as he slowly took the karaoke machine out on the deck.

"Turn the volume up so we can hear you clearly," I said as

he closed the screen door behind himself.

"But I don't know what to say, I can't just start cursing. That'll sound stupid!"

"Yes it does sound stupid, but since you seem to have a habit of sounding stupid, we will let everyone else know how stupid you can sound. Please turn up the volume."

I ran and snatched the index cards off of the kitchen counter, went to the deck, slid the glass door open and handed them to him. His mouth dropped and his eyes blurred with tears when he saw the cards. He let out a loud groan and slowly plugged the machine into the outside outlet then turned it on.

He started out real low and cautious, making sure no one outside could actually hear him. He placed his lips close to the microphone and whispered, "Shit! God-dammit! Go to hell! Mother-fucker! Fuck you! Bitch! Kiss my ass! I hate you!"

Quasim, Travonté, and LaCrystal were holding their mouths and stomachs as they rolled on the floor laughing. Travonté was laughing so hard tears were running down his cheeks as he turned a deep shade of red. Darrin came home from work and looked out on the deck for a few minutes and after surveying the situation, he shook his head and said, "Boy, haven't you learned you can't win with her? She won't give in and you won't win, so just change. Stop acting up."

"Mom, you're crazy," Quasim said through snorts of laughter. "This is a Kodak moment."

"Yes, I'm crazy enough to go to the extremes to teach all of you that you have a responsibility to use appropriate language and you can't talk to people any kind of way." I told them as I sat down at the table, moved the scrambled eggs around on my plate and yelled, "Louder sweetie, I can't hear you!"

Desmond growled the profanity into the microphone. I could hear the embarrassment and frustration in his voice as he spoke each curse word. I went into the kitchen to start cleaning. I could see him pacing back and forth on the deck with the microphone in his hand, dragging the machine behind him. A few neighborhood kids rode up on their bikes, looked up at him on the deck, whispered amongst each other, and rode off laughing.

Everyone wanted to spend their Saturday afternoon in the house watching this spectacle. After 15 minutes, Desmond was allowed to take a 5 minute break, get water, juice, iced tea, or whatever he wanted to drink and then go back to cussing. When he came inside, he set up the karaoke machine in the center of the living room and continued cussing.

Each time his siblings walked past him, they shook their heads and laughed. His face turned a deep shade of red as he hung his head while mumbling profanity.

Eventually, after 30 minutes and a cup of water, his words became flat and monotonous. They started sounding long and drawn out, as if he were heavily sedated. I watched him laboriously repeating, "Shiiittt! God-dammmmmit! Go to hell! Mother-fuccccckker! Fuuuuccck yooou! Biiiitch! Kiss my aaaass! I haaaate you!"

I approached him and asked him if the profanity was out of his system and we made an agreement that this would be his last performance as a "Potty Mouth." I ended the punishment and put away the karaoke machine. Most of his profanity was limited, but every once in a while, he let out a cuss word or two.

Chapter 10
A Can of Whup-Az'

"Hello Mrs. Chambers. This is Ms. Johnson, the eighth grade school counselor. I have your daughter, LaCrystal in my office because she became very distraught over a verbal altercation with a few female classmates. There was a lot of back and forth over who LaCrystal is and is not allowed to befriend. At this point, I think it would be best if your daughter went home for the rest of the day. Actually, I think it would be best if you kept her home for a couple of days—

"Excuse me, but what is this about? Can I speak to my daughter?"

"Mrs. Chambers, as I said before, she's very upset and in no condition to talk right now. Apparently, she and some girls have been getting into spats over trivial things. Five or six girls took it upon themselves to band together and unfortunately, because your daughter did not join their group when the invitation was extended to her, she became a victim.

"From what I'm piecing together, they've been harassing and bullying her for a few months, but she only came forth recently. We didn't inform the parent's because we thought it was just a phase that would play itself out. But the group has gained momentum and now we're intervening."

"Ms. Johnson, why do you keep calling this a group, when it's a gang?"

"You're right. We're looking into classifying it as gang activity. Anyway, they were using things like name-calling, picking and verbal threats. We tried to isolate her from other classmates, but it didn't work. Now, physical abuse has taken place. I spoke with LaCrystal and she said she didn't tell you because she didn't want you to get worried."

My thoughts and emotions were all over the place. I felt the anger rising within me and a migraine was causing my head to pulse. My chest was heavy, like a thick, wool blanket was covering my heart, as I imagined my daughter's pain and fear. I knew that if she took it upon herself to involve the school counselor, her spirit was broken and the situation was detrimental.

"Mrs. Chambers, I called five of the main instigators to my office, including the ring-leader and her cousin. I've tried numerous conflict resolution methods over the last two weeks, including one-on-one counseling and peer mediation, but these girls are out to get your daughter. I couldn't talk any sense into them and I don't foresee reconciliation in the near future.

"There's a lot of envy involved. Strictly off the record, these kids hate her because she dresses nicely, she's pretty, she's smart and the little boys are attracted to her. Personally, I believe when LaCrystal refused the ring-leader's invitation to join their group earlier in the semester, it was a blow to their self-esteem and I must inform you that I'm very concerned for your daughter's safety."

"Have any of the other parents been called? Who are these students anyway?"

"Mrs. Chambers, I am not at liberty to disclose that information to you because they're minors. It seems as if the ring-leader has been using an online Chat-Room to stir up discord towards your daughter. Two students showed me computer print-outs that were exchanged and even though none of them was to or from your daughter, they were all directed at her. The ring-leader and her cousin have very strong influence among their peers and they're using this as a weapon.

LaCrystal has said she hates coming to school."

"I'm sure teachers knew or suspected something? Why didn't they email parents?" I angrily demanded.

"We're trying to get to the bottom of this situation now, but I will tell you this in complete confidence, threats have been made stating the girls are coming to your neighborhood to beat your daughter up for talking to a boy in science class."

I closed my eyes. I could hear my breathing becoming erratic as my eyes became hot behind the lids.

"Mrs. Chambers, you have every right to call the police if any of these students show up on your property. I would hate to be in your daughter's shoes. LaCrystal has been warned by the group, not to talk to any boys, and she is not allowed to have female friends. Anyone caught befriending her was told they will suffer the consequences. Supposedly, they have made a pact not to invite her to parties or sleepovers, because they say she's too stuck-up."

"I can't believe all of this has been going on and no one informed us!" I yelled in the phone. "Can I press criminal charges against these students, because my daughter will not run and cower like a defeated animal? But here's a suggestion, how about suspending the students who are physically harming her?"

"Because when she's being taunted, kicked or her hair has been pulled, it's usually a group of kids behind her and she doesn't know exactly who did it. Are you going to allow her to stay home for a few days?"

"I will take over from here. She will be back in school tomorrow, don't you worry about her. Thank you and goodbye."

I hung up. The conversation was only enraging me. Great big *Alice in Wonderland*, uncontrollable, drowning tears plopped on my desk. I hung my head, and with puffy eyes, snot flowing but you still can't breathe out of your nose weeping, I released my frustration. When it seemed like every water channel in my body was depleted, I prayed, then called Darrin.

LaCrystal was lying on her bed facing the wall when I got home. I wanted to talk in a rational and controlled manner so I waited a few minutes before approaching her and went into my bedroom. Darrin was lying across our bed quietly staring at the ceiling.

Putting my purse down before going into LaCrystal's room, I sat on the edge of her bed and rubbed her back. She slowly turned around. Her beautiful bright almond shaped eyes were blood red and nearly swollen shut from crying. She was looking at me through slits. I gasped and the dam broke. I grabbed her, pulled her into my arms and we cried hysterically as Darrin peered into the room then began pacing back and forth in the hallway.

"I'm going up there tomorrow! I'm going to hurt somebody! I'm not putting up with this shit!" He shouted.

"You're not going anywhere except to jail if you go up there ranting and raving like a lunatic. Let me talk to her and you go calm yourself. I'll talk with you in a little while." I yelled. I took a few deep breaths to regain control of my emotions before redirecting my attention to LaCrystal.

Darrin stormed back into our bedroom and slammed the door. I knew he was in turmoil, but I had to focus on our daughter at the moment. After several minutes of releasing pent up emotions, I pulled the bed sheets and wiped her face. She had experienced the broken, now it was time to rebuild and move toward healing.

"Mommy, I never did anything to any of them." She bawled and laid her head on my lap. "Those girls are already having sex and have been messing with boys since the sixth grade, so when they asked me if I wanted to hang out with them, I refused because I don't want to be associated with that. Since then, they've been picking on me, every day. They say I think

I'm better than them and call me an ugly red rooster because my hair is red. I can't help how I was born. A boy asked me to go steady and when I turned him down, he called me a lesbian and a dirty Cinderella. He said I think I'm a princess, but I'm just a poor uppity girl." She covered her face with her hands and screamed, "Mommy may I please go to another school? You don't know how it feels. I just want to die. I would rather kill myself than go back to that school and go through this every day."

My heart felt like it was being ripped to pieces. At that moment, I made a choice to not allow envy, bullying, depression, suicide, or somebody else's wicked little monsters destroy my daughter. I lifted her face and kissed her swollen eyelids.

"Baby, don't ever feel like you cannot come to me and talk to me when problems overwhelm you. You're not alone. It's okay to be afraid when kids are mean to you and bullying you, but you can't let your fear of them overcome you and dominate your life. Dying is *never* the answer to problems and no human deserves so much power that they steal your joy and your reason for living." She attempted to look up at me as her crying tapered off.

"No, there will be no dying today, darling, not as long as I have strength in my body. You're my gift from God and you have a lot to live for. I'm not giving up on you." I rubbed her hair and wiped her face with my hands. "Those kids have stolen too much from you already. It's time to reclaim your life."

I went into the bathroom, got tissues and returned to her bed. I stood beside the bed and held the tissue gently to her face as she blew her nose.

"Mommy, it hurts when people hate you for no reason. These girls go around and try to get everyone to be mean and spiteful like them and whoever doesn't follow them gets treated badly."

"LaCrystal, the only thing free on this earth is love and hate. People will love you for absolutely nothing and people will hate you as soon as you walk into a room, whether you did anything to them or not. You will always have haters. You have to learn to use that hate, let it make you stronger. And just because those little girls are having sex in the seventh and eighth grade that doesn't make them better than you. It only makes them used and misguided. As long as the girls are allowing boys to use their bodies, the boys will keep participating until they're ready to move on to the next naïve classmate. Unfortunately, the girls won't realize this until it's too late and those same boys won't even speak to them in high school.

"You can't change who you are, so if anyone has a problem with your image, you tell them to take it up with the Creator. You were formed in my belly and made in God's image. It can't get any better than that. Don't ever allow anyone to make you feel like you're less than them. You have a purpose on this earth, so don't give up on yourself before you've had a chance to start living.

"You don't need to alter your hair, change your appearance or your clothes. Your uniqueness makes you special, and I'm not talking about the short-bus type of special either." She let out a hearty laugh.

"As for you talking to classmates, you talk to anyone you choose. There is no royalty in America and you will not be bowing down to those little heifers."

She covered her mouth and muffled a laugh. After nearly two hours of encouragement, I was reaching her and she was gaining confidence. That is when I gave her instructions that I will never regret.

"Pumpkin, we will pray for your classmates, but that doesn't mean they're entitled to hurt you. They don't get a free pass. You have every right to defend yourself.

"When I was growing up, we had bullies too. My mother

taught us to seek out and target the leader. She told us to talk to the leader when no one else was around and you'll see a different type of person. The ring-leader is usually the weakest link. They used their mouth to become the leader and they use their mouth to coerce others to do their dirty work. When you go back to school, don't start any trouble, but if the ring-leader or her cousin lays a finger on you, I give you my permission to open up a "can of whup-az."

She fell back on the bed and shook with laughter.

"Turning the other cheek was good and I'm proud of you for trying to avoid confrontation, but now it's time to turn around and slap the cherry lip-gloss off of somebody's mouth."

"But what if I get suspended?" She asked between uncontrollable laughter and hiccups.

"I'll deal with that. You just focus on getting your homework done tonight. I'm going to talk to your Dad before dinner."

I stayed up praying and keeping watch over her throughout the night. The next morning, I was too exhausted to go to work, so I gave LaCrystal a pep talk and a kiss before sending her off to school. I received a call from the school counselor two hours later. She told me she understood why I told my daughter to fight back and she didn't blame me. She proceeded to inform me that the school's camera recorded LaCrystal and a classmate being followed down the hall by the gang. The ring-leader yelled that LaCrystal had on an ugly fucking shirt, than she ran up behind your daughter and with her fists, pounded LaCrystal in the back.

LaCrystal screamed out in pain and fell to the floor. She grasped a heavy science book in her hands and as she stood up slowly, she brought the book up with her and slammed it into the ring-leader's face. As blood flowed from her opponent's nose, the antagonist fell backward and a fight ensued. It took three teachers to pull LaCrystal off of the ring-leader. When the girls were eventually separated, the ring-leader stood bleeding, shirtless, braless and crying hysterically as her friends pointed and laughed. I drove to the school to pick-up my daughter.

Both girls were suspended for a week. The gang disbanded abruptly and the individual students were never a problem again. I entered LaCrystal into therapy and paid closer attention to her friendships. We also spent a lot more mother-daughter time together.

Chapter 11

Lunch Bully

I was sitting at my desk eating a tuna sandwich when the incoming email message chimed on my computer. I opened it and read the message. Desmond's teacher was complaining that Desmond was being stubborn, difficult, and rude in school.

The message said Desmond and a select few other boys would descend upon students in the cafeteria to reach the front of the line. After gobbling down their lunches, which was usually in a matter of minutes, this little mob searched out passive and mild-mannered victims, male or female, and approached the chosen tables. Desmond specifically, would place his entire palm on the victim's dessert and proceed to ask for it, while his co-conspirators giggled. If the student refused to give the dessert away, Desmond proceeded to smash it with his hands.

I was appalled. Disbelief was the first thing that came to mind, but experience and reason told me the teacher was not mistaken. If she took the time to email me during class, she was at her wits' end and the situation was probably out of control. Here I was teaching my oldest child to overcome bullying and my youngest child was being a bully.

Oppositional Defiance Disorder, Bully Disorder, Lost His Mind Disorder, or however a psychologist wanted to label this act of defiance and disrespect, I knew that ultimately it was Desmond's choice to either continue acting out of control or behave responsibly. He could stay in therapy or on medications until he went through his midlife crisis if that was necessary, but for now, I was about to make sure this never happened again. I emailed the teacher back and reassured her that the problem would be handled expediently.

I prepared dinner that night and made all of Desmond's favorite foods: fried chicken breast strips, sweet corn on the cob, seasoned green beans, dinner rolls, raspberry flavored iced tea and warm Dutch apple pie for dessert.

While cooking, I called each of his siblings into the kitchen individually and secretly explained to them what took place at Desmond's school. I told them I would need their help in pulling off one of my "99% Effective Correction Methods." They all laughed and agreed because they knew this would be another memorable moment in our household, and they were not on the receiving end.

A short while later, I fixed plates and called everyone for dinner. Desmond was intentionally called last. Each person entered the kitchen smiling, took their plate into the dining room, and sat down to say their grace.

Quasim was the first to get out of his chair, reach over and take Desmond's ear of corn off of his plate. Desmond sat dumbfounded. He looked at me to make sure I witnessed what had just taken place.

"I need more rolls." Travonté said as he got up and took Desmond's hot dinner rolls. Desmond's mouth popped open and he widened his eyes. I felt a little sympathetic as I watched those beautiful brown eyes fill with tears, but I knew I had to follow through with the plan.

"Are you going to just sit there and let them do this?" He screamed at me. While he was yelling, LaCrystal reached over, took his iced tea, sipped it and smiled.

"I'm real thirsty," she innocently said. "I know you won't mind."

"Oh my God," Desmond screeched, "You can't tell me that

you didn't just see that! Everyone is taking my food and you're not doing anything. What kind of mother are you?" He threw himself to the floor and kicked the walls. He pounded his heels against the floor. I remained calm and continued eating, all the while praying for patience so I would not snatch him up off the floor and smack him silly.

"Why are you letting them do this, it's not fair?" He screamed in exasperating breaths from down on the floor. He was beginning to hyperventilate so I slowly put down my fork and acknowledged him.

"How does it feel son? You're hungry but people just came along and took your food off of your plate and ate it in front of you; and you can't do anything about it. Your teacher told me that you and some other students have been doing this during lunch. Now that it's being done to you please let us know how it feels?"

He continued to lie on his back and began kicking the floor and crying loudly. I went back to eating and waited another 10 minutes for him to finish his tantrum before I looked down at him again. He lay on the floor, exhausted and breathing rapidly. With his legs and arms stretched out, he lay motionless.

"I want you to think about how those other students felt when you did this to them. Then I want you to think about how you can correct this situation and never cause anyone to feel so humiliated again."

Sitting next to me, Quasim laughed, smacked, drooled, and slobbered all over the ear of corn. "Quasim! Please shut your gluttonous mouth! You sound like a herd of wildebeest feasting in a field."

"Have you ever seen a wildebeest?" He asked sarcastically, "Has anyone ever captured one? Are they in the zoo?"

"Just shut your trap when you chew and eat like you were taught an ounce of manners."

Desmond slowly sat up and leaned against the wall. His

breathing had slowed down to a normal pace. He wiped his face with his sleeve then placed his hands in his lap and lowered his head. He was defeated.

"Are you angry?" I asked him in a soothing tone.

"Yes."

"Did it hurt deeply when someone violated you by taking the food you were about to eat?"

"Yes."

"Do you think you owe your classmates an apology?"

He slowly lifted his head, looked at me and said, "I didn't care how my classmates felt, but now that it's been done to me, I think I know how they felt."

"What do you think we can do about this in the future so that no one else has to experience this type of helplessness?"

He lowered his head and thought for a few seconds. When he lifted his head and looked at me, I could see a difference in his eyes. He finally understood the entire concept of why I had to go to such extremes.

"I can go back to school tomorrow and apologize to them and stop taking people's food."

Thank You, Lord Jesus, my son understands, by golly, I think he's got it. And thank you for giving me patience so I didn't lose my mind on this child. I silently prayed.

"Sweetie, get up and go in the kitchen. Look in the oven and get the additional plate that I prepared for you. I believe you have learned a valuable lesson."

His face lit up as he got up. He went to the oven and retrieved the additional dinner plate. He came back, lowered his head, said grace, and ate his dinner silently.

Everyone stared but no one laughed or ridiculed him over his lesson. They knew they would be held accountable for their actions too. I have never received another email or call about Desmond bullying anyone else, ever again.

Chapter 12
Picasso's Understudy

"Quasim, please come upstairs!" I shouted down to the family room where everyone was watching TV. He entered the kitchen with a wary look on his face. I gently took him by the shoulders, turned him around, guided him to the guest bathroom and pointed to the toilet.

"I'm not a doctor and I never asked you for a fecal sample. This is the eighth time this month, and yes I've been counting, that I've attempted to use the powder-room and I had to look down at stinking, turds floating around in the toilet like bobbing turtles. How hard is it to touch the little shiny silver knob and flush?"

"So what, I forgot." He snapped.

"You say that every week. I got something for you the next time you leave that mess in the toilet!"

He rolled his eyes at me and went back downstairs. I flushed the toilet, put on rubber gloves, sprayed bleach all over the outside and inside of the toilet, got down on my hands and knees and proceeded to thoroughly clean the entire bathroom.

A week passed before I attempted to use the guest bathroom again. I lifted the lid and came face-to-face with turtle turds. I slammed the lid shut, closed the door and ran upstairs to my craft bin, all the while mumbling and fussing under my breath. After grabbing white construction paper, a brown and green marker, pencils and tape, I came back downstairs and placed the items on the kitchen counter. I sat on the stool and drew the oval shape of a toilet bowl, as it would look if someone were peering down into an open lid. I left the drawing face up on the counter, placed the markers next to it, and waited for Quasim.

Hours later he came bursting in the front door and ran straight to the bathroom. I was in the kitchen making a snack, and heard him as he came out without flushing or washing his hands. As he was about to touch the front door to return outside, I came out of the kitchen.

"Oh no you don't buddy, not today. Come back here right now. Flush the toilet and wash your hands!"

He jumped. He was startled and caught red-handed.

"What are you talking about?" He snarled with much attitude.

"You will not leave any more turds in the toilet. I'm sick and tired of going behind you flushing and cleaning. I don't get paid to test toilets and housekeeper is not on my resumé."

"I was about to flush."

"Yeah right, and I was about to throw you a birthday party hosted by the Philadelphia Eagles."

"Man, this is crazy."

"You haven't seen crazy yet buddy. Come into the kitchen!"

I guided him to the countertop and pointed to the markers, construction paper and tape.

"I would like to help you remember what your poop looks like on a daily basis."

"What?" He looked at me with raised eyebrows.

"I need for you to go into the bathroom, wash your hands, take a good look at your poop, then come out here, draw it and color it."

He stared at me blankly, turned up his nose, snatched the paper and markers, rolled his eyes and walked into the bathroom, shutting the door behind himself. He came out a few minutes later, rolled his eyes again and placed the drawing on the counter.

"You better pray your eyes don't get stuck in that position

and you go blind, because I'll guide your nasty little butt into a tree just for the heck of it."

I wish I could charge them a dollar for every time they rolled their eyes at me. I would probably be able to retire early and move far away from all of them.

"I already know what it looks like." He angrily replied, standing above me.

"You should, as how many times as you've left that crap floating in the toilet."

I stared at his drawing. Rolling his eyes, he asked me if I was done. At that moment, I was thankful those mutant powers were not gifted to me or I would have zapped him right out of his boxers. Instead, I looked down at the drawing again, which incidentally, was not half -bad. Just as he was about to walk out the front door I called him back into the kitchen.

"You forgot your signature Picasso. Every great art piece needs a signature."

He stomped back into the kitchen, snatched the pencil off the counter, signed it, rolled his eyes at me for the umpteenth time, turned around, and went outside. I took the drawing, taped it to the inside of the bathroom door and left it there for several weeks, he refused to go in there, and I had no need for any future artwork.

Chapter 13
Roll the Dice

One winter morning, I was looking through a *Family Fun* magazine while at my doctor's office and I came across an interesting chore cube. The cube shaped like the dice gamblers use to shoot crap. It listed chores for family members on each side. The magazine included instructions for making a personalized version. Of course, I had to take it a step further. Would this book be as interesting if I followed the rules and guidelines?

I tore out the page, took it to work the next day, measured the pattern and made my own cube. I invented the "Punishment Cube." It was made up of six even squares. On each side I typed in a punishment, instead of a chore, and added reference to a Bible verse. I was giddy with excitement as I printed, cut, and glued the pieces together. I took the cube home and introduced it to everyone at dinner.

I explained that if any one allowed a disagreement to escalate out of control or become physical, they would have to 'roll the dice' and follow the instructions that were rolled. If they rolled the same punishment, the last person had to roll again. Everyone snickered as they passed the cube around and read it. I told them that if anyone disagreed with the punishment they rolled and refused to fulfill the duties, they would not be allowed to play sports in the fall and spring because they would forfeit their required sports physicals.

Quasim smirked as he read out loud, "Clean out the refrigerator then read Hebrews 12:5-9. How hard can that be?"

He sarcastically asked and handed the cube to Travonté.

"Oh, did I forget to mention that each person has to roll, but the cleaning punishments must be performed as a team. You must help each other."

"What the heck?" Travonté blurted out, as he rolled it in his hands, reading each side carefully. "Wash out all inside and outside trash cans, then write Psalms 103:1-22."

After reading the punishments, he turned up his nose and passed the cube to Desmond. "What is all of this supposed to do?" Travonté flippantly asked as he sucked his teeth and rolled his eyes, "I mean, what is the purpose of it?"

"It's supposed to kill two birds with one stone. One goal is to teach you to work together and the other is to teach you some life principals. Is that okay with you?"

Unfortunately, I already had an idea of who was going to be the first to roll.

"What is Proverbs 22:1-6?" Desmond asked as he turned the cube over and over. Reading then rereading each side before looking to me with a puzzled look.

"I am sure each of you will have a chance to find out." I calmly stated.

Desmond handed the cube back to me, pondered a thought for a few seconds then asked, "How many times can we roll?"

"Shut-up!" Quasim snapped. "Shut-up before she gives us more."

Desmond, ignoring Quasim, asked, "Psalms 146:3-10 is short. Some of these are short and some are long. Why?"

"Some of them have to include certain verses for you to understand the full meaning."

LaCrystal, who had been silent the entire time, finally picked up the cube. She looked it over slowly. After reading each side, she shook her head and placed it on the table.

"Woman, you have way too much time on your hands."

I ignored her and began eating my dinner, but every so

often, I glanced up and caught the boys peering at the cube as they quietly ate.

A few days later snow was falling in large clumps for the second time in a week. There was no school and the boys were bouncing off the walls, leaving holes in the drywall in various places, as they attempted to burn off repressed energy. They got up early in the morning and began the day fussing. Someone demanded to know who drank the last of the milk and now the next person could not eat cereal while someone else was accusing the other of stealing their socks. They bickered constantly, from sunrise to sunset.

Eventually, sometime during the day, they made it outside to play and fight in the snow, returning only when they got hungry. After gobbling down whatever was microwavable, they went back outside until the cold became unbearable. My anger rose steadily as I listened to them come in the house and drop their dirty, wet clothes on the floor. After taking a shower, they ate then went to watch TV, and fought through every program.

I was going nuts. Darrin, who is usually immune to the arguing, finally got out of bed and yelled downstairs once or twice for them to stop fighting or go to bed.

As each day ended, Darrin and I went to bed exhausted and restless. We woke up each morning short tempered and irritable. As luck would have it, the snow kept falling.

One night, immediately after dinner, as if on cue, fighting erupted in the family room. It was time to put my plan into action.

"Ouch," Desmond yelled, "I didn't hit you that hard."

"Try it, just try it!" Travonté threatened.

"I hate you!" Desmond shouted and went into the bedroom, slamming the door behind him.

I went downstairs to the basement with the cube in my hand. The TV was blasting a Skittles commercial. Three kids sat on a beautiful rainbow high above the earth eating the candy.

One starts to question his faith in the rainbow. When he voices his doubt to his friends, the rainbow opens under him and he falls, tumbling to the earth. I was having an attention deficit moment as I stood there thinking of dropping one of my kids from that same rainbow, until Desmond opened the bedroom door and screamed at the top of his lungs that he hated Travonté for trying to take over the TV. Back to reality, I had had enough.

I calmly walked to the hall closet and pulled out a pair of large green *Incredible Hulk* boxing gloves that growled when they came in contact with objects and a pair of red amateur boxing gloves. I called both of them over. They quietly stared at the gloves, at each other, then at me. I handed them each a pair.

"Get dressed. Make sure you dress warmly, and bring the gloves with you." They were still looking at each other, dumbfounded, as I walked away.

While they were putting on their clothes, I placed the cube on the dining room table and went up to my bedroom. After putting on snow boots, two pairs of sweatpants, and Darrin's warm down-filled Eddie Bauer coat, I intended to be out in the cold for a while, I grabbed my metal whistle and went back downstairs to call them up. As I opened the front door and led them outside, I could hear them behind me a few paces, whispering.

"Now you did it," Travonté snarled through clenched teeth, "You done made her lose her mind."

"No I didn't, you did," Desmond snapped. "You just have to keep stuff going all the time."

"This is crazy." Travonté yelled at my back as we approached a clearing in the open field a few yards from our house. "What is the meaning of all this?"

I kept walking towards the clearing then stopped in the center and slowly turned to face them. They stopped in their tracks and huddled protectively together.

"Since the two of you can't seem to understand that no one wants to hear fussing and arguing every night, and because you don't seem to care that it stresses us out, I think it's time both of you get all of that energy out of your system."

They continued to stand in one spot, near enough to hear me and far enough to break into a run, just in case I truly had lost my mind. I could see them through the falling snow looking at each other with bewildered expressions.

"Since you are determined to keep fighting, I am going to give you the opportunity to pretend for fifteen minutes that you are Tyson and Holyfield, you choose your opponent."

Quasim came out on the front porch to watch the scene. LaCrystal peeked out of her bedroom window. Darrin came outside in his pajamas and looked across the field at us, then went back into the house.

I walked over to a specific spot and told Desmond that this was his corner. I went approximately fifteen feet across and designated Travonté the opposite corner. I stood in the center and yelled their ages, weights and alias, in my best announcer's voice.

"When I blow the whistle, you have ten seconds to reach each other. You must stop when the whistle is blown the second time and return to your designated corners. No hitting below the navel or above the neck. That will disqualify you, and that means automatic 'lock-down' and early bedtime for a week." On lock-down, our children are not allowed to watch TV, go outside, attend sleepovers, or enjoy any type of leisure. They are only allowed out of their bedroom to eat, shower and use the bathroom. It was the ultimate hourly punishment.

"Let's get ready to rumble!" I shouted in my fake Cronkite voice.

They scrunched their faces up like they couldn't believe I was having them do this. I put one hand up to confirm that the whistle was about to blow. They rushed to their imaginary corners and put on their boxing gloves. I blew the whistle. They began slipping and falling in the snow as they attempted to run toward each other. They never made it. I blew the whistle after a few seconds and told them to go back to their corners.

"You have to run toward each other like warriors. It's too cold out here to be pussy-footing around! We need movement people!" I was enjoying this. "When we go back inside I don't want to hear anymore foolishness or I'm likely to turn Spartan on you. So let's start over and release all of that energy."

I blew the whistle. Again, they began slipping and falling in the snow. Just as they reached each other, I blew the whistle. Ten seconds were up. They walked back to their designated corners.

I know they felt foolish (which was my goal) after each attempt left them on their butts or on their faces in the snow. I giggled as I watched them sluggishly stomping in the snow, stopping every few minutes to shake the snow out of their pant legs or out of the gloves. I intentionally blew the whistle every time they got within an arm's distance of each other and sent them back to their corners. After five or six whistle-blows, I allowed them to reach each other for two seconds. Desmond's *Incredible Hulk* gloves let out a loud growl when he swung and made contact with Travonté's shoulder. They both fell to the ground rolling in laughter.

When they finally sat up and stopped laughing, they were covered in snow so we went inside. I had them sit at the dining room table after changing their clothes as I explained to them how irritating it is for parents to listen to screaming and fighting all day. A home should be a place for relaxation, peace and serenity, like a retreat, not a war- zone.

Instead of having so much free time to fight, they rolled the dice and spent the next few days working together completing the chores and writing Biblical essays with no more than three errors per page.

By the weekend, they were too exhausted to fight. Friends were ringing the doorbell to see if they could come out and play football in the snow, so after painstakingly reading and discussing their Bible passages, they anxiously apologized to each other. When I nodded in appreciation, they were out the front door in seconds, nearly tearing the handle off as they slammed it shut behind themselves.

Chapter 14
A Series of Unfortunate Pets

"**M**om." Travonté exclaimed, as he burst in the front door, "Guess what I found?"

"I'm not sure, but it better be legal, alive, and minus a leash." I laughed as I pulled items out of the refrigerator that were taking on their own life forms. With Darrin at work, I planned to spend a nice summer Saturday afternoon thoroughly cleaning all kitchen appliances, inside and out, and hopefully resting for a few hours.

He reached into his pocket and pulled out a long, pea green colored snake. I let out an ear piercing scream as the snake slithered up his forearm towards his elbow.

"Get it out of here!" I screamed. "Get it out now!"

"But Mom," he pleaded, "it's just a garden snake and he's nice. See." He stroked the snakes' back and the forked tongue searched his arm, as it slithered closer to his neck.

"Can I keep it?"

"Have you lost your mind? I hate snakes!"

"But Mom, it doesn't have any teeth?"

"How the heck would you know that are you a vet?"

"But it's a garden snake and they don't bite."

"Where did you get your zoology degree?" I asked, pointing to the front door.

"I'll keep it under my bed."

"No you won't, that thing could get loose and bite someone in their sleep."

"Aw Mom, it's a nice snake and I'll take good care of it."

"No you won't be taking care of it. Nature will, because it goes back outside." I pointed to the door again. "Outside! Now!"

Sulking, he turned and went out the front door, all the while talking to the snake and telling it that I was a big 'meanie.' I went back to cleaning the refrigerator. This boy stepped right out of a Huckleberry Finn novel; every day was an adventure and I never knew what to expect.

A few hours later, he was running back in the house again. This time he held up a large, beautiful, yellow and black lizard. I nearly fainted.

"Please Mom," he begged, "I need this lizard to add to my zoo."

"What zoo are you talking about?" I leaned against the kitchen counter, as far away from the lizard as I could get.

"I opened a zoo with two of my friends. It's in one of their garages. We collect animals and charge kids $2.00 to see them."

My head ached at the temples. Was this one of those instances that Darrin warned me to overlook and let it run its course?

"How long have you been a zoo-keeper?" I said while turning to arrange items on the countertop.

"We've been collecting animals since early spring," he bragged. "So far we have two lizards, a red bird, a pigeon, a gecko, spiders, a ferret, a raccoon, a snake, two dead cicadas, two cats, a dog, a hamster, two cockroaches, some regular sized roaches, a rabbit, two rats, and a turtle."

My head was spinning like I had stepped off a merry-go-round. I leaned against the countertop. I wondered if the other kids' parents knew what was going on in their garage.

"We tried to catch that skunk and her babies that kept coming in our backyard a few months ago, but she got away," he proudly exclaimed. "My friends will pay double to see a skunk and $10.00 to get sprayed by her or one of her babies. If she comes back, I'm catching her."

Dizzy. Dizzy. Must stop room from spinning.

"Mom, I was outside minding my own business when this lizard caught my eye. I got closer and it just sat there, like it was waiting to be caught. It didn't turn and run or anything. This was God's work. This lizard was meant to be mine."

I looked up at the ceiling and prayed a quick prayer. He kept bargaining and stroking the lizards back. "I'll feed it, buy crickets and take good care of it, I promise."

"Travonté, you can't keep bringing everything you find into the house. All creatures don't want to live with you. Furthermore, they all die after a few months anyway."

"Yes, but that's because they were all dumb. They either got out and the cat killed them, or they got too close to the heat lamp and committed suicide. Those pets just weren't too bright."

I kept thinking about picking and choosing certain battles. I did not want another pet in the house, but I knew that Travonté would desperately keep searching for anything unlucky enough to be in his path.

"Go ahead and keep this one Travonté, but you must do extra chores to pay for the crickets, or whatever it eats. And I better not see that thing upstairs," I warned. "Do you hear me?"

His eyes bulged with happiness as a smile spread across his face. He attempted to come towards me for a hug, but I quickly put up my hand stopping him, I was not about to hug a lizard with a boy attached.

"Oh yes, thank you Mom, thank you so much. You won't regret this." He exhaled and ran downstairs to the family room with the lizard cradled in his arm like a newborn baby. While he was cleaning out the empty aquarium for his newest pet, Desmond came inside and went downstairs. I waited and listened.

Within the hour they were fighting over who would be the

primary caretaker of the lizard. Travonté kept telling Desmond to stay away from the cage because his toxic breath would kill the new pet.

Before the night was over, they were scuffling, pushing and yelling at each other over lizard duties. I yelled downstairs and reminded them that if they continued, they would have to roll the dice. They stopped immediately.

A few days later Desmond came inside with a snapping turtle he had found in a creek and asked if he could have a pet, too. I was apprehensive, but after persistent begging, I agreed to let him keep the turtle.

Within a few hours, they were fighting over whose pet was smarter, smelled the worse and moved the fastest (neither pet would win a race against a snail).

Two weeks after the pets moved in, Darrin was watching TV in bed and I was reading a book, when Travonté and Desmond came bounding up the stairs to our bedroom.

"Mom," they yelled in unison, exhausted and out of breath.

"Mom, guess what!" Travonté yelled over Desmond. "You don't tell it, it's my lizard."

"So, I noticed it first and I told you."

"So, it's still my lizard," Travonté gloated and rolled his eyes at Desmond. "My lizard is a girl and she just had six babies."

"Are you kidding, that was a pregnant lizard? That's probably why she didn't run when you tried to catch her."

"Yep," Travonté beamed. "The baby lizards are in the cage right now."

"I saw her have the babies," Desmond said with a smirk. "And only I know how she had them."

Travonté intentionally shoved Desmond out of the door space.

"Don't start that mess." I warned them.

"It's my lizard, and I'm going to name all of them," Travonté proudly boasted.

Darrin slowly looked up from the TV, to study them.

"If you continue fighting no one will have a lizard, babies, turtle, or anything else. I'll personally release them back in the wild."

They looked at each other and silently decided that the fighting was not worth losing a mother lizard and her babies.

"Desmond, you can have one of the babies if you want one." Travonté eagerly offered. "Mom, can you and Dad come downstairs and see my lizards?"

I was tired, but I decided to go down and look at the new family. As I was standing up, I saw Travonté intentionally squeezing Desmond out of the doorway again.

"Travonté, stop pushing him, when you act mean, mean things come back to you." I placed my book on my pillow as they turned and ran down the stairs, fussing, pushing, and fighting all the way to the basement. It was going to be a long weekend.

"There are only five now." Desmond shouted as he placed his face to the glass peering into the aquarium.

"What are you talking about?" Travonté demanded, pushing him away from the cage. "Let me see."

Travonté pressed his face to the aquarium counting the baby lizards once and then again. He looked up with tears in his eyes. "Desmond it's your fault, you left the cage cracked."

"No I didn't! You fed them last."

"Stop fighting or get rid of all of it, the aquarium included!" Darrin yelled as he entered the family room. They quieted down.

"Both of you start looking for the baby lizard and shut the top of the aquarium." I cautiously peered into the cage. The five remaining lizards were black and green and actually cute. I knew the cage would eventually not be big enough for all of them. I wanted to bring up the subject of releasing them, but decided it wasn't a good time.

They searched for hours, looking under sofa cushions, inside the fireplace and on bookshelves. Desmond found the baby hooked to the cat's claw. He and Travonté wrapped the baby in paper towels and buried it in the back-yard after a small memorial.

A few days later Desmond came running up to me and graphically told me how he watched the mother lizard eat one of her babies instead of the crickets. That same week, another baby went missing. Then the top of the cage was left cracked and two more escaped and were killed by the cat. Within a month, all of the babies had mysteriously disappeared, escaped, or were eaten. We made Travonté release the mother lizard. It was clear he was not ready for the responsibility of caring for pets.

Days later Desmond decided to give his pet some fresh air. After sitting the turtle in the backyard he went to play with friends. He returned hours later and entered the kitchen with a sad expression on his face. The turtle ran away.

I know it was wrong, but this was one of those moments when all of that nurturing maternal crap went right out the window. I laughed until tears ran down my face. That turtle was the only pet with enough sense to make a break for it and was never seen again. Desmond rolled his eyes at me and walked away.

A few weeks later I was looking out the kitchen window and saw Travonté running down the sidewalk with Desmond in tow.

"Mom, Mom!" Travonté yelled as he entered the house.

"No! Whatever you have, want, snatched, stole, saw, dragged home or found, the answer is no!"

"But we trapped the mother skunk I won't bring her in the house I have her in the backyard and I don't want you to frighten her and cause her to have an accident."

"Boy, if you don't get that funky skunk out of my backyard,

I'll bust you upside your head so hard you'll still be dizzy on your wedding day. You better let that thing go now!"

"Aw man." He sucked his teeth and sulked out the front door. Desmond followed. They stood on the porch for a few minutes.

"Let's go search for some wild bobcats." Travonté suddenly exclaimed, and the pair was off again in search of more unfortunate pets.

Chapter 15
Bubble Bath Dilemma

"When you come in for the night, do not go sit in the family room and watch TV." I shouted over the rail. "Go take a shower, it smells like a barn down there."

I waited and listened. After a few minutes I yelled again. "Shower, please!"

Silence. I knew whoever came inside went directly downstairs to the family room because I could hear the TV playing. I saw a quick image flash in my mind's eye of Desmond sitting on the sofa sweating, stinking, and scratching as mud dripped from his clothes.

Causing a loud raucous, I stomped down the stairs. Upon reaching the lower level, I could hear frantic movement as someone came running out of the family room. Leaves and dirt were in his hair, his shirt and jeans were torn, he was wet and covered in mud. His socks were a filthy, dingy grayish-brown and caramel colored sweat or muddy water was dripping from his face. Desmond was an eleven year old real-live "Pig-Pen."

"Boy, did you hear me tell you to get in the shower?" I snarled through clenched teeth.

"Yes, but I was watching this program first."

"Desmond, you can't sit around with those filthy clothes on—and what is that smell?" I pinched my nostrils closed and tried to talk in quick breaths so the atrocious odor would not go into my mouth.

"I was in the creek catching lizards and turtles."

"Son," I muffled, continuing to cover my mouth to keep out the smell and stop myself from gagging. "You're covered in mud. Take off those clothes and throw them in the trash, I don't want that filth in my washing machine, and then get in the shower. You can go back to watching TV afterwards."

As I headed upstairs I could hear the shower running. Lately, he had been skipping showers and going directly to bed, sometimes fully dressed in the clothes he had played in all day.

When he was younger, he wore the same underwear for so many days that on the fourth night, it was time for me to enforce hygiene. On this particular night, I shook Darrin to wake him, but after a few seconds of lip smacking, gurgling and some alien-like sounds, he rolled over and snored loudly. I was on my own.

Creeping down the stairs and entering the boys' bedroom, I stood at the foot of the bunk beds. Reaching under the rail of the top bunk, I tapped Desmond lightly on the shoulder.

"Did you take a shower?" I whispered.

"No," he groggily answered.

"Did you brush your teeth?"

"No."

"Did you shower yesterday?"

"No, my clothes were dirty, but I wasn't dirty. Why do I have to take a shower every day anyway?"

"Did you play in the grass, the creek, and the dirt today?"

"Yes."

"Then get out of bed right now and shower!" I shouted, scaring the Heebie-jeebies' out of him. He jumped up, hitting his head on the ceiling and scrambled down the ladder and into the bathroom.

On this particular night, I had an uncanny notion to go back downstairs. I went and waited in the hallway for him to exit the bathroom. The shower was running, but I could hear no movement; no dropping the soap, slapping of wet feet on the bottom of linoleum, or adjustment of the faucet, just water running down the drain.

I pressed my ear against the door, trying to follow Desmond's movements. He was standing near the bathroom sink singing. I stood up and slowly cracked the door. He was fully dressed in those filthy clothes, looking in the vanity mirror, popping pimples and singing rap songs.

Swinging the door open, I stomped over to the shower and without saying a word, turned the knob downward. I went to the cabinet, pulled out bubble-bath, and poured some in the tub.

"If that's for me, I hate bubble-baths."

"Good. I hate dirt, so we're even."

I walked over to the laundry closet, pulled out a clean towel and wash cloth, and told him to wrap the towel around his waist.

"What!" He turned a deep shade of crimson. "I'm not getting undressed in front of you. You're crazy. I'm too old for you to bathe me."

"You're absolutely right. You have five minutes to strip out of those filthy clothes or I'll undress you myself."

"You're not undressing me." He raised his voice and grabbed his jeans by the loops.

"I hope I don't have to undress you. The choice is yours."

"I don't need a bath." He yelled, squeezing the loops even tighter between his fingers. "Who made you the ruler of when I need a bath anyway?"

While he was babbling about hating baths, showers, and anything pertaining to water, I grabbed the bottom edges of his shirt and began pulling it over his head. The forced movement caused him to bend over towards me. He stretched out one arm at a time and allowed the shirt to be removed then immediately clutched his jeans again. I bent down, pulled off each mud-caked sock, and placed the towel over my shoulder.

"You're not the boss of my body. I should have some inalienable rights in this freakn' family too."

I was tempted to grab a handful of bubbles and throw them

in his mouth. I gave him one more chance to cooperate, for I was not about to liberate him from bathing.

"If you were born in the 1400's when bathing once a month was acceptable, it would probably suit you, but I'm not King Henry and you're no peasant so I'll turn my back while you take off your jeans and underwear, get into the tub and wash yourself."

He backed up, his face now turning pomegranate red, and looked at me with pure hatred emanating from him. "I'm not getting in that tub. I already told you that my clothes are dirty. I know when I need a bath."

I wrapped the towel tightly around his waist and warned him again that he could willfully get undressed or I would take him by force.

"It's not fair, it's not fair, damn it!" He shouted as he slowly stepped out of the jeans, keeping on his underwear.

I took him by the shoulders and directed him to the tub. I knelt, put my arm in the water up to my elbow and tested the temperature.

It was at this moment that he began shouting profanities, tussling, swinging his fists, and growling like I was performing an exorcism. He was determined not to get into that tub.

Somehow, I was able to get a firm hold on him after a few minutes. I quickly pulled down the boxers, all the while dodging his swinging fists. It was as if my mind foresaw his movements prior to his lashing out. Within seconds, he was naked with a towel around his waist. I ripped the towel away, picked him up, and plopped his body into the tub, splashing water and bubbles everywhere.

I encouraged him to cover his private area as I washed him. He cupped both hands over his genitals, looked up at me with daggers in his eyes and shouted into my face,

"I already told you that I have inalienable rights to stay dirty in a democratic society if I want to. It's my right as an American citizen to stay dirty if I please. I'm not hurting anyone."

I looked at those tempting bubbles again, before continuing to wash his upper torso and leaving. Upstairs, Darrin was peacefully snoring in a pool of drool. As I crawled into bed, I elbowed him to interrupt the snoring.

As for the little politician, I never had to force him to make friends with soap and water again. He willfully bathed regularly, and even splashed on cologne every so often.

II.
Middle School:
You Better Act like You Know

Chapter 16

Vigilante Feline

I spent the entire winter warning fourteen year old Quasim to stop harassing Ameré, the family cat. Let her be the queen of her domain, she's not bothering anyone, I told him. All she did was sleep in the sunbeams, watch birds, and chase flying insects that entered the house. But he continued throwing items and kicking at her when she got close to him. I was constantly picking up Tupperware lids and other miscellaneous items lying on the living room floor that he had apparently thrown at her. When approached, Quasim quickly denied responsibility.

After weeks of this treatment, whenever he entered a room, Ameré would back into a corner, flatten her ears, and begin to hiss and cringe. It was obvious he was provoking her and I intended to catch him in the act.

One morning as everyone was busy preparing to leave for work and school, I quietly crept downstairs. Ameré was backed into a corner at the front door and Quasim was swinging a wooden hanger at her. Hissing in fear, she frantically searched for an escape route.

I crept up behind him, grabbed his collar, opened the front door and shoved him out, slamming the door behind him. He steered clear of me and the cat for a few days, but eventually went back to abusing her when he thought no one was looking.

As the seasons changed and warm weather approached, we would soon find out that Ameré had her own plans for revenge.

I was in the kitchen one beautiful spring Saturday afternoon preparing eggplant parmesan for lunch while Ameré drank water from her bowl in the corner. Suddenly she bolted from the kitchen, ran to the foyer and crouched beside the front door.

A short while later Quasim came strolling down the sidewalk dressed in jean shorts and a white t-shirt. I peered out from the kitchen. Ameré's back was hunched, her ears flattened, and a deep, mesmerizing growl ending in a high pitched howl slowly emanated from her throat.

Quasim casually entered the house humming a tune on his iPod. He shut the front door and froze as his eyes locked on Ameré. He glanced toward me in the kitchen, searching my face for an answer, as if I were going to intervene. I had nothing but wide-eyed fear to offer.

"Arrgh!" He screamed as he turned around and tried to reopen the door, but each time he pulled the knob, the bottom edge of the door hit the tip of his shoe and slammed shut. He was trapped. He let out a mezzo-soprano scream and attempted to run past her. She cornered him, circling like a predator, hissing, baring her teeth and lashing out with claws extended, daring him to run.

I stood perfectly still. I was not about to play referee with an angry, vigilante cat and have her turn on me. This was their battle and I wanted no part in it.

Quasim tried to cautiously maneuver his way up the foyer steps. Big mistake. Ameré stood on her hind legs, released a ferocious screech, and attacked his lower legs. Within seconds she had swiped him numerous times with her front claws, leaving long, bloody marks on his lower legs. He was yowling and looking for an escape route. I ran and jumped up on the kitchen countertop and prayed he did not seek safety in there with me.

"She scratched me. She scratched me." He yelled running past me, on his way to the basement. Another big mistake. As he cleared the first set of steps, Ameré leaped off the top stair and landed on the top of his head. Peeking around the corner, I hopped down and followed them.

As she ripped into his scalp I cringed in horror. He slammed his body into the walls like a pinball machine in a vicious attempt to shake her loose. She slid down to his back, leaving long open slits in his neck, revealing white flesh against his Hershey colored skin. I covered my mouth, afraid to scream, yet, too morbidly curious to look away. The shouting, screeching and howling made it difficult to distinguish who was in more agony.

Red stripes appeared on his t-shirt, as he continued to violently buck and thrust the cat off his back. In a last effort, he waved his hands wildly and slammed his body into the bathroom door, dislodging her. He quickly shut the door behind himself.

"You need to get rid of that cat!" He bawled hysterically. "I'm not coming out as long as she's out there."

Ameré lingered in the hall, growling, swinging her bushy black tail back and forth and pacing in front of the bathroom door. When she was sure he was not coming out, she slowly climbed the stairs. I ran and jumped back up on the kitchen countertop, pulling my legs to my chest. She walked past me, stopped, acknowledged my presence then went back to her water bowl. Gradually, I came down from the counter and continued cooking.

More than an hour later Quasim finally came out of the bathroom and cautiously came up the stairs, sniffling and examining his wounds.

He peeked around the corner searching for the cat before entering the kitchen. I checked his injuries, and even though it looked like he had fallen in a rose bush, none of the scratches and cuts required stitches or hospitalization. I put peroxide and Neosporin on the open slits in his scalp, on his neck and on his back. His legs received the worst blows and were covered in bandages.

As I attended his wounds, I reminded him that all of this was consequences for his actions.

After her fill of water, Ameré strolled past us. Quasim cowered by the sink, but she walked right past him and went into the living room to take a nap. He wore pants for the rest of the season and never bothered the cat again, except to make every effort to avoid her.

Chapter 17
Copacabana

LaCrystal walked up and down the cosmetics aisle in the local Wal-Mart. I watched as she looked longingly at the lipsticks and eye-shadows and eventually had to be pointed to the Lip Smackers and tinted gloss collections. She was a maturing eighth grader and wanted to express her creativity, unfortunately, tinted lip gloss was as far as I was willing to allow a thirteen year old to creatively express herself.

One fall night she entered our bedroom and asked to play in my make-up. After being given permission, she went into the master bathroom, closed the door and began humming a tune.

A short while later, she opened the door and smiled. Heavy purple, green, and brown mixtures were on her eyelids and mixed in her eyebrows. Firehouse red lipstick, which I was not aware I owned, covered her lips and in a haphazard attempt, she had applied self-adhesive black eyelashes. One lash was higher than the other and as she flashed a big smile revealing lipstick smeared all over her front teeth and blinked her eyes repetitively, the lash flapped up and down like a butterfly in flight.

"Mommy, how do I look?"

"Like a hot mess."

"Whatever!"

She shut the door, only to rip it open a few minutes later. With her eyes squeezed shut and arms flailing, she screamed, "It burns. Get it out, get it out!"

I ran past her and into the bathroom, snatched Kleenex out

of the box, and directed her to the toilet. As I removed a glob of black liquid eyeliner from the crevice of her eye, she moaned and clung to my shirt.

"What were you trying to do?"

"I was rushing. I'm sorry. I was rushing to put on liquid eyeliner and it dripped in my eye."

Her eye instantly became red and puffy, remaining that way for the rest of the day. Wiping the cosmetics from her face with Pond's cream, I told her about the infatuation she had with make-up since she was a toddler, and the fiasco it led to.

"When you were three years old, my best-friend visited from South Carolina. She owned lots of expensive make-up, like M·A·C, Clinique, Flori Roberts, Fashion Fair, and stuff I could barely pronounce. All of it came in pretty containers, velvet tubes and cute little boxes."

LaCrystal listened intently and held the wet cloth to her eye. I sat on top of the bathroom countertop.

"One evening while you were taking a nap on my bed, my friend and I sat in the living room catching up on stories from our old neighborhood. After some time went by, I went to check on you and found that you were no longer on the bed. We searched everywhere. There were only a few places a three-year old could hide in a one-bedroom apartment.

"Every minute that I could not find you, it became harder and harder to breathe. I was beginning to hyperventilate as I shouted your name over and over. The apartment was beginning to feel like an incinerator. Sweat ran down from my breast, tickling my stomach and my armpits itched from perspiration mixing with my deodorant, my vision was blurred and light-headedness caused me to stumble around and I felt so lost and helpless. We lived on the fourth floor of a government subsidized high-rise building that should have been condemned—

"Why did we live there then?"

"I lost my job, and my apartment, and was left homeless when you became ill with ongoing respiratory infections in your lungs and had to be hospitalized numerous times. After telling a friend of my predicament, she encouraged me to contact a social worker, who put us in a room at the Pitts Motel Homeless Shelter in Northwest, Washington, D.C., but when the staff found out about your hospitalizations, they rushed me into the first apartment available and it was better than walking the streets every day, so I didn't complain."

"Where was Darrin?"

"We were separated because he'd made some bad choices that could have destroyed our relationship."

"But couldn't you forgive him so he could help us get a better place to live?"

"Sometimes, it's not that easy LaCrystal. Can I finish telling the story?"

"I was a single mother, on welfare, living in the projects and attending Strayer College through a government subsidized program. It was one of my lowest periods, but, I set goals, stayed focused and allowed my hardships to strengthen me, rather than break me. After Strayer, I got a full-time job in the federal government and enrolled at Howard University, but we still couldn't afford to move.

"Arthur Capper Dwellings, the housing project where we lived, was one of the worst in D.C. Heat and water didn't run through the buildings, but roaches and rats ran through the hallways and greeted you like pets. I never invited classmates over because the smell of urine and the sickening chemical-cottony odor of burning crack-cocaine on every floor were nauseating. Furthermore, I never knew when a semi-conscious, half-dead, drug addicts body would be sprawled out in the hall or on the elevators, and I didn't want to take the chance of preparing people to duck-and-run if gunfire rang out. Many nights I had to pull my mattress on the floor so we could sleep away from the windows—

"Why didn't you call the police?" LaCrystal interrupted, "I would've called anonymously."

"I couldn't afford a house phone and cell phones hadn't been invented. People used pagers or beepers, but even with those, you still had to locate a phone to call the number that appeared on the pager. Once or twice, late at night, after bundling you up and walking two blocks to the corner store, I called the police. They came, hung out, laughed and joked with the drug dealers, hustlers and the tenants who housed them, and then left."

"Did anyone ever bother you? Were you scared to live there?"

"Yes, but I relied on common sense and street knowledge to survive."

"What do you mean?"

"I knew the unspoken rule. This was the late 1980's and early 1990's when crack cocaine hit D.C. and nearly destroyed the black community. The police weren't protecting tenants, so I had to do what was necessary to stay alive, which meant, keep my head down and my eyes averted when witnessing a drug transaction, a gang beating, or a murder.

"But what happened to me when I was lost?"

"Huh? Oh yeah, I'm sorry. I lost my train of thought."

"We needed to look out the window, which was covered with blankets, sheets and cardboard boxes to shield against the cold and to cover the torn screens. I could not bring myself to look, so, my girlfriend looked out the window and confirmed that you had not fallen to your death. She suggested we call the police, but I continued to cry and pull clothes out of drawers, flinging them everywhere. I went to the closet dumped out my clothes hamper and noticed in the farthest corner of the closet, a small doll-sized figure covered in dirty clothes. It reminded me of the clown sitting in the corner in the movie, *'Poltergeist.'*

I walked over and pulled the clothes off of the figure. You had piled clothes on top of yourself to hide. I pulled you out, and yelled to my girlfriend. Clutched tightly in each of your little chubby fists were two tubes of her expensive lipstick. The tubes were rolled up and some were broken in half. There were maroon, red, brown and coral colors on your hands, lips, teeth and forehead. On your legs and arms were lipstick drawn circles and you were squeezing the broken brown color between your thumb and forefinger."

LaCrystal leaned back on the toilet and laughed hysterically as tears rolled down her cheeks.

"I squeezed you to my chest and bawled like a baby. When I took you to the bathroom, I could hear my friend fussing as she inspected her cosmetics case. She was furious for hours, but eventually, she forgave us, even though she didn't visit again for another three years."

"I still like to feel and smell lipsticks." LaCrystal beamed.

"I know, but you're only in eighth grade, so that cancels make-up for a few more years."

We ended the night sitting on the floor watching classic movies until bed time.

But come on readers, you already know it will never end that easily in this book. Let's keep reading.

A month later, I took a day off from work for a surprise mother-daughter outing. Waiting in the car, I watched as the school bus pulled into our community and LaCrystal stepped off. She turned when I blew my horn.

The flying cockatoo hairstyle was one issue. The shimmering, disco sky-blue on her eye-lids, the black mascara and eye-liner so thick around her eyes she could have been mistaken for a raccoon, and that fire-engine red lipstick on her lips, almost sent me into cardiac arrest. Thank God she was not dressed provocatively or I would have caught a felony charge.

She noticed me sitting in the car then bolted down the street to the house, slamming the front door behind herself. I followed in the car. She was already upstairs in her bathroom vigorously rubbing tissues in circular motions in a failed attempt to wipe off the mascara when I entered the bathroom. Black tears ran down her rouged cheeks, mixing with the assortment of colors causing her to now resemble a melting wax clown-raccoon.

"LaCrystal. You deliberately went into my bathroom, used my make-up, and walked out of this house looking like a broken-down *'Lola at the Copacabana,'* even though you knew you weren't allowed to wear it yet—"

"Everyone else is wearing make-up, and I'm the only eighth grader that's not." She interrupted. "I'm tired of looking like a big baby and wearing stupid pony-tails all the time." Her breathing was erratic, her face was flushed and she was beginning to hyperventilate.

"I get good grades and I do everything that you tell me to do. All I want is to 'not' look like a baby anymore." She hiccupped as she sobbed uncontrollably into her colorful hands.

I felt a little sorry for her. She was trying to take a stand. Too bad, flexibility was not on my agenda.

I took her shoulders, directed her to the toilet and began removing the black smudges from around her eyes with Kleenex and Vaseline while thanking her for her honesty.

"Sweetie, you don't need theater make-up to be beautiful, God gave you natural beauty. I won't compromise my rules and I expect you to respect them as long as you're living under my roof. When I feel you're ready, sometime in high school, I'll teach you how to wear it correctly."

She eventually calmed down and agreed, but in high school she discovered that most of the girls wore little or no make-up. Needless to say, my cheap make-up sat in my bathroom growing hard and old and useless.

Chapter 18
Spiderman

I left my desk for ten minutes, only to return and find three voice mail messages on my phone. Desmond was at school jumping off chairs and standing on tables. I played the messages a few times, listening to the weariness in the middle school teacher's voice, before writing down everything. I sat quietly and breathed deeply for a few minutes. I knew it was my choice to allow another one of his outrageous episodes to upset me and raise my blood pressure, or I could turn the tables on him and force him to bring logic and reason to his impulsive behavior.

Arriving home hours later, I took off my shoes, placed my purse on the counter, washed my hands, and turned the radio to the gospel station. When Darrin came home from work, he entered the kitchen. I handed him the note and we talked about the upsetting situation as I prepared spaghetti for dinner. Our conversation was interrupted by an emergency call from his job and he had to return to work, but asked if I needed his assistance before leaving. I kissed him, reassuring him that the problem would not overwhelm me, furthermore, I knew Desmond was in the basement, making as little noise as possible. He already understood consequences were in order for his outrageous behavior.

While cutting onions, garlic cloves and green peppers, I prayed for patience and guidance. After sautéing the vegetables in olive oil, I felt a little more at peace. I called Desmond upstairs. He entered the kitchen, grinning and sniffing the strong Italian aroma while craning his neck to look into the simmering pan.

I asked to see his hands. I rotated the wrists from front to back, then back to front, and held them up to the light and studied them with the intensity of a skilled surgeon, then rubbed my chin and shook my head. He had a perplexed look on his face.

Not finding any markings, holes, or punctures on his wrists, I asked, "Where does it come from?"

"Where does what come from?"

"The goo son, where does it come from?"

"What goo? I never saw any goo."

He held his hands close to his face and checked his wrists.

"You know Desmond, the web slinging goo? Where in the heck does it come from? I can't find any holes."

He quickly realized this was going to be another learning lesson and began explaining his version of the incident. While he was babbling about playing tag during class, Travonté walked in. Before he could put his books down I called him into the kitchen.

"Excuse me Travonté, but can you take this stool and sit it out in the backyard, somewhere in the center of the grass?"

"Huh?" He asked with raised eyebrows.

"Can you please place this stool in the center of the backyard?" I haltingly repeated, pausing after every word.

Travonté responded with a sideways glance, but since he was not in trouble, he quickly took the stool and did as I asked. I turned to Desmond, hugged him and walked him to the glass door leading to the deck.

"Now son, since you dream of playing Spiderman, I am going to give you the opportunity to perfect your web-crawling, web-slinging, and imaginary leaping across buildings. The stool is placed out back for you. You may crawl, jump, fly, cartwheel, trapeze, dance, or sit on it for thirty minutes, but I want you to get all of that energy and disobedience out of your system so no teacher has to ever call me at work with this type of disciplinary problem ever again."

The whining and tears were right on cue. "Do I have to? My friends will see me. Can I take another punishment? I'll stay on lock-down for a month—I'll let you beat me? Please don't make me go out there. People are already laughing at us because of all of the weird things you make us do as punishments. Why can't you just get a belt and beat me like a normal parent?"

"No son, I want to make sure your teacher never has this problem again."

"I won't do it again, I promise."

"Hurry outside, because for every minute you are not out there, you owe me a dollar."

"What?" He screamed. "That's crazy! You're crazy! I'm not paying you to jump over a stupid stool."

"But thinking you're a Spiderman web-crawler is rational and sane?"

"My teacher doesn't like me."

"She doesn't have to like you, she has to teach you, and in order to do that, she needs a safe and controlled environment and you're about as controlled as a puppy."

"She's always catching me when I do something. She waits for me to act out so she can set me up. I'm telling you she doesn't like me."

"That's okay, because right now I don't like your actions either. Now take that noise out back and web-crawl." I gave him a slight push toward the door.

He dropped his head and went out, slamming the screen door behind him. I heard him mumbling that he hated everything and everyone as he walked to the stool. He sat on it for a few minutes before crawling up on the top, standing on the wooden round seat, and positioning his arms in a flying Superman position. He tucked his head and jumped.

"While you're out there, I'll get the dictionary and we can draw up one of those petition letters to the school board and explain how they need new rules to accommodate you."

I ran upstairs, grabbed my camera, and snapped some pictures of him leaping off the stool. Darrin returned home and went directly to the glass door leading to the deck. He looked outside at Desmond, shook his head and then turned and went upstairs to take a shower.

After thirty minutes I called Desmond inside to check his progress. As he walked past everyone with his head down and the kitchen stool in his hands, Quasim snickered, Travonté shook his head from side to side, and LaCrystal repeated, "Lord, Lord, Lord."

Desmond placed the stool in the kitchen and sat on it. I sat beside him and showed him the drafted letter:

Dear Virginia School Board,

My son, Desmond, feels your rules are too strict and that they limit his creativity. We have included a new list of rules that would make his life much easier:

- *Gum and candy should be allowed all day.*
- *Homework should never be given over the weekend.*
- *Physical Education should be two-class periods.*
- *All male students should be allowed an additional free breakfast and lunch.*
- *Academic classes should follow lunch and physical education.*
- *There should be no tardy bells.*
- *No student should be written up, especially Desmond, when he is diving, rolling, sleeping, cutting hair, and web-crawling in class. All of his ridiculous behavior should be tolerated.*

Sincerely,
Desmond and his lovely mother

As he read the letter a second time, I got up and went to the stove, giving him a chance to evaluate the punishment, and seasoned the ground turkey and cooked it. I waited a few more minutes to address him.

"Did I miss anything?"

"No."

"Would you like to add to the list?"

"No. I'm sorry," he sighed. "I don't want to do this anymore. I get the point that you're trying to make, but I have gym before this class and it's hard for me to settle down."

"Son, medications can help you settle down. If you need help with ADHD or some other undiagnosed mental condition, we can look into trying medications again."

"No. No more meds. Please. I'm sorry. I'll try harder tomorrow."

I walked over to him, pressed his head against my stomach, ran my hands through his thick, black curls and thanked him for understanding his actions and the consequences in a mature manner.

"I don't like slipping out of my Christian-hood or getting stupid with punishments, but teachers have a highly stressful job and since the bulk of my taxes goes towards education, I want to make sure you're receiving the best that the public school system has to offer." I endearingly told him. "It's impossible for anyone to learn if a teacher has to pry a kid off the walls. You can play Spiderman for Halloween, but it's off limits in school."

After dinner, I told him to go downstairs and think about his actions. He slowly walked toward the stairs with drooping shoulders. Suddenly he stopped and turned around.

"Mom, can I write the teacher an apology letter?"

"That would be an excellent and very responsible idea. I am very proud of you for thinking of that option."

Folks, needless to say, there were no more Spiderman episodes.

Chapter 19
Sock Trolls

"Lord, tell me this child is not sitting in church, in frigid temperatures, with no socks on his feet." I whispered as I closed my eyes and opened them again. Crap. He was indeed sitting beside me with pale, ashy ankles peeking out from his high-water pant legs. I leaned over. "Desmond, where are your socks?"

"I don't know."

"What do you mean, you don't know?"

"I couldn't find any of my socks for two days."

I leaned back and tried to concentrate on the rest of the service but was clearly distracted by those ankles.

When we arrived home, the first thing I did was kick-off my shoes and yelled to the boys as they headed down the stairs to their room.

"I want all socks upstairs in 30 minutes. Bring dirty, clean, holey, mismatched and brand new. I'll be waiting."

I could hear hushed whispers, accusations, fussing, and dresser-drawers opening and slamming shut, as they argued over which socks belonged to them.

They came up stairs with one or two pairs of filthy socks, and three or four mismatched socks. Travonté carried three pairs of clean, white socks. Quasim had one pair of white and a few pairs of black. Desmond carried a single gray sock and a brownish-gray sock (both were originally white). They dropped the bundle in the center of the floor. I had to hold onto the kitchen counter to steady myself, everything began rotating and shifting around me.

"I know you're kidding." I demanded. "We spend money holidays, birthdays, and every school year on socks, and—you guys are kidding me, right? Is this a joke?"

They stood in the kitchen looking down at the small miscellaneous pile on the floor.

"You're supposed to wash clothes every weekend, so why are you bringing up filthy socks? You need to go back downstairs and locate at least five pairs of socks apiece, or we'll spend all Sunday washing clothes and searching the house for socks."

I walked past them and went upstairs. They went back downstairs mumbling, whispering, and fussing again.

They returned soon, each with an additional dirty sock and said they did not know what happened to the others as they began placing blame on each other. I told them not to worry, I would catch the culprits. They got quiet and with wide eyes looked at each other.

"You see," I said very seriously, "it's nobody's fault that the socks are missing. Even though you take them off and throw them everywhere except the dirty clothes hamper, it's not your fault."

Their eyes danced in anticipation and they smiled when they thought the blame would be placed on someone else.

"Shhhh, here is the problem." I whispered to them, concealing my mouth, leaning towards them as they huddled around. Darting my eyes, I whispered loudly, "We have miniature sock-trolls."

They popped their eyes and gasped, then quickly looked around the kitchen.

"I plan to stay up tonight and catch one running through the house stealing your socks. If I catch it, I'll hold it so you can see it in the morn—there's one right there!" I screamed and pointed to the bottom of the stove. Pushing and shoving, the boys ran over and scanned the cracks and crevices in an attempt to see tiny trolls running around with their dirty socks.

"You nincompoops! There are no sock-trolls. Lord, I am blessed with a family full of geniuses. Put your filthy socks away and stop throwing them all around the basement, then stealing someone else's. Geez."

I rolled my eyes and turned away from them as I opened two packs of blue-raspberry Kool-Aid and poured them into a pitcher. This was going to be a long day.

They grabbed their mixed up socks and went back to their room. In the future, we insisted they purchase socks with the money received for birthdays, Christmas, chores and as gifts. If anyone's socks disappeared, they were given permission to wear my nylon knee-hi's, and guess what, the socks stopped disappearing.

Chapter 20
Suit Boy

The middle school teacher sounded extremely weary as she told me that Desmond had been throwing pencils across the classroom. When asked to stop he mumbled under his breath and ignored her.

Three weeks earlier, I had made a pact with Desmond, hoping to encourage him to control his impulsive outbursts and disregard for authority. If he could go for four weeks without any disciplinary referrals, he would receive a video game sleepover complete with pizza, soda and snacks.

My children knew I had little tolerance for disrespecting school officials and adults. I never minimized or overlooked this behavior, so when they acted out, they knew the consequence that would follow, they had to wear, "The Suit," which was usually a dress shirt, tie and slacks, but sometimes a full three-piece suit was in order, followed with an apology letter to the teacher.

Arriving home after work, I went straight to my closet, pulled out the ironing board, the iron, and spray starch. I took the arms load to the dining room and set up before going to Desmond's closet. After picking out a nice lavender shirt with gold cuff links, black dress socks and a pair of black slacks, I asked him to turn off the TV and come upstairs.

Pointing to the items on the ironing board, I sat on the stairs.

"Son, you know what is expected of you."

"But I don't know how to iron."

"Inexcusable. You didn't know how to cook either, but you

learned or starved. You didn't know how to ride a bike, but you kept falling until you learned. You couldn't swim at one time, but you splashed around for many summers until you taught yourself."

"I don't care about ironing. I'll wear my clothes wrinkled. I'm not ironing that stupid crap."

I could feel anger rising in me, so I took a deep breath. I was determined to stay calm. There was no need for me to be upset because regardless of what he said or did, he paid no rent, paid no bills, bought grocery or financially took care of himself. So whether he liked it or not, he was in violation of the house rules and would be held accountable, starting with learning to iron the clothes he would be wearing the following day.

I went upstairs and got one of Darrin's dress shirts and took it downstairs. I plugged the iron into the nearest outlet and proceeded to show Desmond how to put water in the back and explained which buttons to push for an ample amount of steam. I showed him how to read the label in his clothing and set the iron temperature to match the material. The entire time, he kept rolling his eyes up to the ceiling and sighing real loud.

I continued by explaining where cuffs and creases belonged. Personally, I thought that this should have been Darrin's job, but, bills have to be paid, food put on the table, and clothes on their backs, so, while he worked late, I sucked it up and did what I had to do. After several minutes of disrespect that I was tiring of ignoring, I proceeded to look up at the ceiling too, maybe he saw a crack or a funny shape like people see in the clouds.

"Yeeep!" I said with an intentionally long and exaggerated drawl, making a pop like the hollow of a popping cork as I sat down on the bottom step and sounded the letter "p." I smiled a broad smile. "We will definitely need a new coat of fresh paint."

Desmond looked at me and rolled his eyes so hard they could have gotten stuck backwards in the sockets. His disrespect was extremely annoying, but he was highly proud of playing this game with me. I wondered which of us would succumb first.

"I was not looking at the paint, thank you very much."

"Yeeep." I popped again with the same southern drawl. "How many gallons do you think we'll need?

He exhaled a large sigh of defeat before getting up and approaching the ironing board. I got up and continued the demonstration.

When we were done, he hung his clothing on a hanger to save the creases and placed them over the closet door for the following day, then he wrote an apology letter to his teacher.

I wish it were that simple, but as you readers are aware, this book is about teaching preteens and teenagers to accept responsibility and changing rebellious and inappropriate behaviors, even when outrageous methods have to be used. So let's keep reading and see how this situation turns out.

The next morning I was not feeling well and decided to take the day off from work. I waited on the stairs for Desmond to come up, intending on inspecting his book bag to make sure he did not sneak in a change of clothes.

He nonchalantly came up the stairs in a football jersey and jeans. When he saw me he nearly jumped a foot off the floor.

I slowly stood up, went to the kitchen, opened the junk drawer, and pulled out a map. Slamming it on the dining room table, I shouted, "Find it!"

"Find what?"

"Find the location," I said pointing to the map.

"Find what location, what am I looking for?"

"Your mind Desmond, because if you think you are going out of this house without those dress clothes on after disrespecting your teacher, then you have lost your mind, you had better find it before I go DMX up in here."

He dropped his book bag, turned around and ran down the

stairs, slamming the bedroom door behind himself.

"The kids are going to laugh at me and start calling me, "Suit Boy," again." He yelled. "And if you make me wear it, I swear, I'll never go to school again!"

Travonté came up the stairs, and as he walked past me and to the front door, he told me that Desmond was in the bedroom tearing up his dress clothes. I ran and quickly got a needle, scissors, and a spool of white thread, then sat back down and waited for him to come up. Humming a Lizz Wright tune, I mentally prepared myself for whatever was about to come.

He came upstairs fully dressed, but had clearly popped all of the buttons and cuff links off the nicely pressed lavender shirt, leaving numerous holes, as it hung loosely open.

"Where are the buttons?"

"I don't know. I don't care about those stupid buttons." He said and rolled his eyes.

He was trying my patience and PMS was not making the situation any easier. I got up, went to the kitchen drawer, pulled out a zip-lock bag, and handed it to him.

"Son, please go and find every button and cuff link that was on that shirt so I don't have to yank your hair into a Mohawk before breakfast."

He snatched the bag from me and ran down the stairs. Ten minutes later, he came back with the buttons inside and shoved it at me.

"Oh, baby I have no need for them. You pulled them off so you're going to sew them back on."

"Are you crazy?" He yelled hysterically. "I don't have time for that shit. I'll miss breakfast."

"No, you're crazy. I just have PMS. So I would advise you to start threading the needle and getting those buttons back on that shirt because I don't like prison food, and you're about to make me catch a charge." I calmly stated.

"I'm not sewing them on."

"Then you can stay home with me today and we'll do this all over again tomorrow."

"I've already missed breakfast, why even go now?"

I told him to take off the shirt and lay it flat on the floor to position it for the buttons. He slowly took the shirt off, but threw it to the floor.

"By the way, if you stay home I need the carpet shampooed and my clothes washed."

"Forget it! I'm not touching your gross underwear."

He dropped to his hands and knees and quickly sewed every button on and put in the cuff links. He put on the shirt, tied his tie, grabbed his book bag and ran out the front door.

"Have a nice day. I love you. Bye-Bye." I shouted after him.

Slamming the door, he ran up the street shouting profanities at me and saying he was never coming back.

He looked mighty fine dressed up, I thought, as I took two Midol, crawled in bed and drifted into a peaceful sleep.

Chapter 21
Plumbing 101

Travonté raced up the stairs and into our bedroom, Desmond trailed close behind. I braced myself and sat up in bed. It was late summer on a Friday evening and I had every intention of having a peaceful weekend, but that thought quickly vanished.

"Ma." Travonté shouted, nearly out of breath, "I just caught Desmond flushing candy wrappers, gum, and paper down the toilet. Remember when you told us that certain types of stuff will clog the toilet?"

Before I could answer, he continued.

"Well, Desmond has been flushing all kinds of stuff. He refuses to throw away his trash."

"So." Desmond shouted in retaliation, peeking from behind Travonté. "I saw you flushing paper towels down the toilet and Mom told you not to do that either."

They went back and forth for a few seconds until Travonté blurted out, "Now the toilet is backed up. Poop keeps circling and coming to the top, and it almost spilled on the floor."

I held up my hand. I heard enough and my stomach was not taking the news too well either.

"There are three people using that basement bathroom and each of you will have to come up with $100 to pay for a plumber to come fix the toilet. Quasim is 14, Travonté, you're 12, and Desmond you're turning 11. You're all old enough to know right from wrong, and whether you agree or not, you made this mess and you will clean it up."

They looked at each other then slowly looked at me.

"I don't use that bathroom and I won't pay one Lincoln to fix it," I calmly reassured. They stared blankly at me, bewildered and blinking every few seconds like animated characters.

"The only other bathroom you will be allowed to use and destroy with items that you already know shouldn't be flushed, is the one in the 24-hour Wa-Wa gas station, which is three blocks away. I'd hate to see any of you messing on yourselves while trying to run three blocks in the middle of the night, so I guess you'll all be holding it until morning, or until you get the money together to fix the problem."

"Can we use Dad's toilet-snake and take turns trying to get items out of the toilet, because I don't have $100," Travonté said and nudged Desmond.

"He's working late, but, I'm sure he won't mind if you use his tool as long as you put it back and don't break it. You may also have a pair of rubber gloves."

Travonté looked at me, his dark eyes bulging, wondering if I were serious or not, then blurted out, "I'm not sticking my hands in no stinking toilet, glove or not!"

"The toilet snake should be in the toolshed, but don't forget boys, the nearest public toilet is three blocks away." I shooed them away and went into my bathroom.

They ran down the stairs, fussing over who would be first to use the toilet-snake and who would use the gloves. I dropped three pairs over the handrail and down to the basement, then went and sat back down, fluffed my pillows and meditated on thoughts of relaxation and quiet while silently thanking God for whoever designated Monday through Friday as mandatory school days. Five full days educators worked with our little ingrates and put up with their nonsense, and yet, they aren't even compensated with a decent salary. I made up my own personal name for the education system, "bass-ackwards," and chuckled to myself.

After meditating myself into a light sleep, Travonté woke me when he came running up the stairs again, with Desmond in tow.

"Ma, we fixed it. We took turns and ended up using the rubber gloves to pull out all kinds of stuff. It's flushing properly now and I don't think any of us will be throwing trash in it again." Travonté beamed.

I smiled and said, "Well, if we agree as to what should and should not go in the toilet, then I believe you've learned your lesson."

They smiled, turned, and ran. The toilet was never clogged again with trash.

Chapter 22
Target Practice

It was a scorching summer Saturday afternoon when I placed several ingredients for Paula Deen's quiche recipe, along with a hope and a prayer, on the kitchen counter. *It would surely be a lot of wasted eggs if this concoction did not come out right,* I thought staring at the array on the counter.

Suddenly, Travonté burst in the front door.

"Ma, Ma." he shouted, trying to catch his breath while waving his hand to get my attention. "Desmond is outside playing with some really bad, older kids!"

"If he ain't dead, dying, dehydrated, unconscious, or bleeding profusely, then I'll talk to him when he comes in," I replied, without turning around. I wanted peace and I was not about to let anyone get me riled up.

"But Ma you don't understand. These boys steal, smoke, get suspended, curse, and bully smaller kids."

"I'll *talk* with him when he comes in."

"But you told us not to hang out with older kids and they did something really bad because the police are out looking for them right now," he pleaded. He was on the verge of tears.

Now he had my attention. I told him to wait in the kitchen while I got my shoes, but before I was half-way up the stairs, I heard him yelling as he ran out the front door, "I'll go get him! I know exactly where he is!"

Darrin was lying in bed taking a cat nap. Waking him, I repeated Travonté's message. He quickly dressed and followed me downstairs with his car keys in hand. He told me to stay at home, in case Desmond decided to show up, while he drove around the neighborhood looking for him.

I sat on a kitchen stool, looked out the bay window, and tried to remember what I had been doing. I turned and jumped when Travonté slammed his body against the front door, forcing it open.

"What the—"

"Ma. Blah, blah, blah, police, blah, blah, Desmond, blah, blah, blah, shot!"

My ears only received fragments of what he was saying before running out the front door and up the sidewalk.

Lord say it ain't so, please say it's a dream. I prayed. Someone was screaming Desmond's name, but I kept running and praying.

As I rounded a corner and saw police cruisers speeding past me and into an adjacent neighborhood, I stopped to evaluate the situation and catch my breath. Realizing the screaming had stopped and it was my own voice, I called on the Name of the Lord and continued to run in the direction of the sirens.

My cell phone began vibrating in my pocket. I slowed my pace and answered it with shaking hands.

"Ma, Desmond and the police are here now," Travonté stated, "and I won't let Desmond leave."

"Is he okay? I'm on my way back." I hung up before waiting for an answer and called Darrin. I told him to come home as I was running back to the house. Police cruisers were everywhere. Officers stood outside their cruisers talking, while others sat in the cars waiting. I ran past them and up the porch steps.

Desmond was standing in the kitchen. He took a step back when he saw me. I grabbed him, spun him around like a spinning top, and inspected him from head to toe in a matter of seconds. I tilted his head up, pushed his thick, black hair away from his face, and noticed the deep crimson indentation in the center of his forehead. Darrin walked in the house and immediately inspected Desmond again.

"They shot him in the face with a bb gun!" Travonté shouted from behind me. "I thought it was a real gun, and I called the police. Yeah, I was the one who called, and now they want to talk to you two."

Desmond began rapidly telling us how he allowed his new friends to shoot him as a joke. He said his friends shot two squirrels, a lady's yipping little dog, and two girls playing in their yard, and when they wanted to practice close range on someone, he volunteered. Desmond slowly sat on a stool.

Darrin stood in front of him, locked eyes, and said, "Son, anyone with a gun aimed at any part of your body is not your friend. That pellet could have hit your eye and damaged it permanently."

Desmond was silent, but I could tell by the glossy faraway look in his eyes, he missed the full understanding of his actions.

"If those boys at 10 and 12 years old are shooting animals and kids what do you think they'll be shooting when they reach ages 18 and 20? Desmond, why do you think I don't allow video games that promote shooting and graphic violence?"

"I just thought you hated video games because *you* can't play them." He honestly replied with a shrug of the shoulders.

"No son, that's not the reason. I don't like where the violence is heading." I told him as I fought to keep my composure. "Every year game-makers enhance the violence and visuals to be as life-like as possible. Why? Do kids really need to feel like they're killing a real person? I have never seen any good come from shooting guns, someone or something is always the victim." My head was pounding and I was becoming angrier every second. "We know people personally who have lost their lives due to gun violence and there isn't a damn thing exciting or fun in death."

I threw my hands up. "If we don't wake up and pay

attention, we're going to create a generation of children with one frightening skill, expert marksmanship. It's happening every year and it's only going to get worse."

"We won't be promoting guns, or joining the NRA, so whatever infatuation you may have with weaponry, you'd better get over it. Quick. Or you can join the military or the police force." Darrin angrily snapped.

"But I told them they could shoot me, and I don't see why everyone is making such a big deal of it,"

"Are you so desperate to be accepted that you will allow people to harm you as long as they pretend to be your friend?" Darrin yelled. "Son, you should never have to compromise your safety, your body, your rights, your freedom, or any—

"The police are at the door!" Travonté interrupted.

Darrin and I went out on the front porch. Officer Crawford, a young blond male of medium build and with eyes the color of cool Caribbean water you see in pictures of the Pacific Islands, told us the police had received several calls that three kids were walking around our neighborhood shooting pets and people. He informed us that he knew the families of the two boys involved, and they were not bad kids, just bored and mischievous. We were told that they 'accidentally' shot squirrels, a dog, and two little girls.

I reminded Officer Crawford that the boy's intentionally shot our son in the face and could have caused serious damage. The officer begged me not to press criminal charges against the kids and put felonies on their records at such a tender age. He said he knew the parent's personally and would be grateful if I would allow him to speak with the other parents before the situation escalated further.

I looked to Darrin, who shrugged his shoulders, leaving the decision to me. I allowed the officer to persuade me not to press criminal charges. Unfortunately, I would live to regret that decision.

Desmond was sent to bed early while Darrin and I discussed the situation. The following day, we sat our 11 year old down and had him write five characteristics that defined a good friend, and for weeks, periodically, we discussed why it is not okay to hang-out with friends who carried weapons, harmed others, or made bad choices. We kept him close to home and a watchful eye on him too.

As for my restless feelings toward Officer Crawford, I personally believe the policeman made a preferential choice, favoring the two little blonde terrorizer's reputation over our son's safety, which was in my opinion racially motivated, but I would soon have another encounter with him and I would confront him and bring accountability to his actions.

Chapter 23

Lip-Popping

"Mom." Travonté yelled, "Call the police!" Sitting at my desk I looked at the caller identification screen. He was calling from home. I listened to his erratic breathing, followed by sniffles. He was either about to cry or had just finished.

"Travonté, what's the matter?" I asked and exhaled deeply.

"Call the police, I'm not playing."

"Son, what is the problem?"

"This girl," he stammered, "This girl hit me in the mouth and busted my lip."

I stifled a laugh.

"Why would a girl just come up and punch you in the mouth with her fist?"

"Two girls were arguing and I wanted to see them fight, so I egged them on. As we were getting off the bus, one of the girls got in front of me and because I was laughing at her she turned and swung her stupid purse. I didn't have time to duck, and it hit me in my mouth. I think she had a brick in there and that's considered a weapon."

"Travonté, you're exaggerating. No girl carries a brick in her purse. How bad is your lip? Is it split? Are you missing any teeth? Is it bleeding?"

"Well it felt like a brick. Anyway, it stopped bleeding and now I want her arrested."

"Travonté, no one is going to jail over a busted lip."

"But she had no right to put her hands or her purse on me.

You told us we're not allowed to hit girls and that's the only reason why I didn't hit her back."

"Put ice on your lip until I get home. And don't go near that girl, we'll go to her house and talk to her parents together."

"That's okay. I'll handle this. I don't want her thinking I had to run home to my mother."

"That's very mature and courageous of you. If you need my help, call my cell phone." I secretly hoped no one would have to pull that little girl off him.

He was waiting for me in the kitchen when I walked through the front door. I tilted his head back and inspected his lips. There was a small slit on his upper lip underneath the pubescent sprouting peach fuzz.

"Mom, I went to her house and the first thing I did was tell her that I didn't come to fight, I came in peace. When she realized I wanted only to talk, we apologized to each other. Mom, I think it would be best to stop meddling in girls personal affairs because they could be carrying anything in their purses."

Chapter 24
Next Stop-the Olympics

Clothed in socks and a backless, cotton, hospital gown, I patiently sat on the examining table and listened as my doctor tried to explain medical terminology. My cell phone began ringing. After the fifth set of calls, I excused myself, went into the hall and answered it.

"Hello," I said with a snappy, irritating tone.

"Hello, Ms. Chambers?"

"Yes."

"This is Deputy Daniels of the Stafford County Sheriff's Department. Is your son named Desmond?"

"Yes."

"Ma'am, I have him in my custody for throwing balls against someone's house and breaking their living room window. The owners have decided not to press charges, but I cannot release your son until a parent arrives."

"Why didn't you call his Dad? My husband has a cell phone."

"Ma'am your son said he preferred to call you. Will you be able to come and get him anytime soon?"

"Yes. I'm in my doctor's office right now, so it will be a while."

"Yes Ma'am, I understand. I will be in the parking lot waiting."

I hung up, leaned against the wall, and squeezed my eyes shut to stop tears of anger as I prayed.

"Lord, this boy is trying my patience. I don't know how much more I can take, he is non-stop. Please control my hands and feet when I see him so I don't go flying through the air like Jackie Chan and kick him senseless. And Lord, help me control my tongue so I don't say some stuff that could send me to hell."

I took a deep breath and went back into the examining room. After apologizing to my doctor for the intrusion, I dressed and left the office.

The officer was standing outside of his vehicle when I arrived. Parking next to him, I got out of my car and verified my identity. He informed me of several vandalism incidents in several neighborhoods involving Desmond and his friends. I was in shock. He told me that Desmond was in their system and becoming a public nuisance.

"But my friend gave me permission to throw balls at his house." He blurted out.

I rolled my eyes at him, "Lord, if this child was sitting on a cloud eating pizza when you handed out common sense, you need to give me a sign, quick." I said to no one in particular as I looked to the heavens. "Y'all gon' make me lose my mind, up in here, up in here." I shouted, quoting DMX's song, *"Party Up in Here."*

"But he said—

"Shut-up and get in the house right now!" I interrupted and pointed in the direction of our house. He sprinted down the sidewalk. I apologized to the police officer, then went home.

After dinner, Darrin and I sat with Desmond for nearly two hours and talked to him about the consequences of his destructive behavior. Whether he heeded our guidance, only time would tell; he was given four weeks punishment and rolled the dice. As the days progressed, Darrin kept insisting I reduce the punishment and I began to wane. I cut the punishment short and Desmond was filled with gratitude, I with doubt.

A week after that disastrous decision, as I stood in the kitchen looking out the front window at two magnificent humming birds feeding on our blossoming tree, out of my peripheral vision I saw Desmond sprinting through the woods. Close behind, two officers pursued on foot. As Desmond increased his speed, ducking branches and weaving in and out of familiar territory, I watched in horror.

Shouting his name, I ran out the front door and to the edge of the woods. Hearing the raucous, Darrin came downstairs and stood on the porch. I went to him and told him what I had just witnessed.

"Oh well, he has to come home sometime," he casually stated, "You come in the house and stop making a scene."

How could he be so nonchalant? I thought as I followed him back into the house. I called our other children and asked them to come home and help look for Desmond. Quasim and Travonté complied, but LaCrystal adamantly stated that she was not spending her Saturday afternoon looking for a 12 year old renegade.

Hanging up the cell phone, I went into the kitchen and began pulling out various items. Two hours later, a mouth-watering array of foods covered the stove and countertops; spicy jambalaya, cornbread, steamed broccoli and iced tea. Satisfied, I exhaled and walked over to the window and peered out. Darrin came up behind me and wrapped his arms tightly around my waist and gently swayed my body from side to side. As we moved in unison, my tension slowly eased and my body relaxed. After several minutes he told me to come upstairs and lie down for a while. As he went upstairs, I opened the oven and was about to put the jambalaya in when the front door swung open with so much force, it slammed into the wall, causing the door stopper to make a springing sound.

Desmond stood in the foyer in a dirty torn t-shirt. Twigs and leaves were stuck in his thick hair and scratches covered his face and arms. Two sweating police officers entered the house behind him with their hands secured on their revolvers. I stood in front of Desmond, blocking his further entrance into the house. My teeth were clenched so tightly my jaw throbbed.

Dazed and confused, he soothingly rubbed his cheek and asked, "What'd I do?"

"Excuse me ma'am," one of the officers asked, "But did you just slap him?"

"I don't know officer, but I think I may have."

"You did?" Desmond asked as he continued to rub his cheek. "I didn't even see your hand move."

"Do you know that I saw you being chased? Can you even imagine how upsetting it is to see your child being chased by police?"

"Yes, but they didn't catch me." He smirked. "And they didn't know my name either, but I knew if I ran home, you'd turn me in, so I just kept running until they got tired of chasing me."

"Desmond, have you lost your damn mind?" Darrin shouted coming down the stairs and addressing the officers. The police then explained that a group of kids were throwing rocks at passing cars. They caught up with a few and they gave the names of all the kids involved, addresses and what each person was wearing. Because Desmond was the only one already in their system for numerous counts of destruction of property, they wanted to talk to him first. When they spotted him walking home and pulled up beside him, he ran, so they pursued him.

One officer turned to Desmond, shook his head and said, "Son, running from the police is not a good thing and can have unpleasant consequences. In the future, if you ever encounter the police, don't run."

"Ye—Yes sir."

"Officer, we're sorry. We'll talk to him and try to get him to understand how grave this situation really is." Darrin assured them as he walked them to the front door.

The second officer turned around as he stepped out on the porch and said, "You've got one hell of an Olympic track star there."

They walked off laughing. That night, we sent Desmond directly to bed after dinner. The next day we sat him down and talked to him for hours about his destructive behavior and how it was spiraling out of control. We tried to make him see that with his name stored in the county police records, they could be building a case against him and he could end up in a juvenile detention center. He quietly listened, but I could tell by his eyes that what was being said was not a priority for him.

In the months to come, he would continue to act out as a neighborhood nuisance. We began dreading the summer months. The nearer the spring, I started becoming irritable and anxious. I knew that summer was right around the corner and our sons were too old for summer camp, and they refused to go anyway, but they were also too young to work. So we were caught in the middle. I tried to find programs for the boys, but they were very expensive and because of our work schedules, we could not get them to and from the summer programs which began and ended while we were at work.

As fate would have it, the following summer, Desmond and two classmates (out of either boredom, rebellion or sheer pre-teen hormonal-stupidity) decided to break items in a nearby neighbor's yard. She filed a small suit and Darrin and I ended up in court. After presenting the case to the judge and asking him to allow us to intervene and teach Desmond a lesson in responsibility, a judgment of $400.00 was placed on the pre-teens record and they were ordered to pay restitution for the broken items.

We agreed that Desmond would work with his father on Sunday nights, cleaning offices for $25.00. Each week, after he received his money, we purchased a money order, had him sign it, address the envelope, and mail it to the courts.

We thought this would deter him from acting like a little hellion. But within a few months, he was at it again. Unfortunately, this final time, the consequences of his actions fell on his shoulders.

Chapter 25

Batman

I sat up in bed. The digital clock read two o'clock in the morning. Did I hear someone scream or was I dreaming? I listened for a few minutes to the silence in between Darrin's snores. Maybe I was dreaming. As I was about to lie back down, I heard it again. Quasim was desperately shouting, "Ma. Ma."

My first thought was an intruder had entered the house. I grabbed the hammer that I kept near my bedside, shook Darrin, told him something was happening in the basement, and reached for my robe at the foot of the bed, as I headed down the stairs.

I prayed that no one was stupid enough to break into our house. Lord knows I didn't feel like sending anyone to meet their Maker. For years, I taught my children that if anyone forcefully entered your home, the odds were they did not break in to eat warm chocolate chip cookies and play Scrabble with you. They came to do harm; to steal, rape, rob and kill, but the unspoken word in our home is we would not be begging for our lives, instead we would commence to beating the hell or the devil, whichever one decided to exit first, out of the individual.

As I ran down the stairs skipping every other step, I could hear Darrin fumbling and cussing as he searched for his shorts. I entered the boy's bedroom and saw Quasim and Travonté struggling over a baseball bat. They pushed and pulled back-and-forth, attempting to rip it out of each other's hands. Tears were rolling down Travonté's cheeks and Desmond was perched over the rail of the top bunk wielding the fireplace poker in his hand like a Roman spear, pointing it directly at Quasim's head, while shouting, "Get off of him! Get off of him, God-dammit!"

"What the—

Desmond and Travonté were attempting to double-team Quasim. I felt like they were about to reenact the 1979 classic movie, *"The Warriors,"* and have an all-out rumble in our basement. Had Quasim not yelled for help, I can only imagine how the situation could have escalated and ended.

"What the hell is going on down here? Desmond, put that poker back beside the fireplace." Darrin's voice boomed as he entered the bedroom a few seconds behind me. He walked over and snatched the bat out of Travonté and Quasim's hands.

"Dad, Quasim kept calling us names," Travonté cried.

"I don't give a damn what he said." Darrin yelled, "Unless you're Batman or you joined a baseball team, I better not ever hear of you threatening anyone with a bat. Kids out in the street call you names and you run in the house and stay inside for days. Now I have to come down here and lose sleep for this mess. I have to get up and go to work in three hours. This shit is selfish and ridiculous!"

"Yeah," I chimed in. "Selfish and ridiculous. They called Jesus names, beat Him, spit on Him, and pulled His hair out of His scalp and His beard, but you never heard of Him picking up a stone or a piece of wood and beating the cow-squat out of anyone."

They stood around looking at each other, sweating, breathing hard, with chests rising and falling in unison.

"There will be no more sleepovers, or any other type of leisure, until all of you learn how to treat your family members with respect. You will not treat your friends like celebrities and your family like trash. That's not happening in this house." Darrin shouted.

"If we have this problem again, all of you can forget about either of us investing our time or our money into supporting you during sporting events. You won't be allowed to play any sports this year," I yelled. They all groaned.

"All of you get in bed right now, and we better be able to hear a church mouse pissing on cotton when we get back upstairs or no one goes outside for a month." Darrin shouted as he went into the family room and gathered all of the fireplace pieces and tucked them under his arm.

We went upstairs, but could hear them whispering as they placed blame on each other.

"Shut your mouths and go to sleep!" Darrin yelled. Instantly it became quiet.

The next day, when they came home from school I pulled out the Punishment Cube. They all agreed to accept the consequences for their actions, mainly because if anyone refused to roll, they received an additional punishment. If they still refused to accept responsibility, I was not about to scream and holler or get physical, they would be given, "A Taste of Chocolate." In Stafford County, Virginia, the sheriff wears chocolate colored uniforms, and if necessary, they would be called in as a last resort to restoring order.

Chapter 26
Saved by "*The Pursuit of Happyness*"

Desmond entered the house with his head down, walked directly into the dining room where I sat at the table reading a Stephen King book and handed me a pink disciplinary referral. Apparently, he had been distracting the entire class by rolling around on the floor while the teacher was trying to carry out the lesson plan.

"Desmond, I don't want to sit on you and force medications down your throat. I believe you're intelligent enough to understand that there will be consequences when you begin to act like you live, "*Where the Wild Things Are*," I quietly told him. "Desmond, did you know that the school can recommend you be placed in a contained environment for students who are uncontrollable and lack discipline?"

"But Mom," he desperately cried out, "I was so bored I wanted to scream. Watching my fingernails grow would've been more exciting."

"Son, you have to learn to make the most of your time. Did you go to your teacher and ask her for extra assignments?"

"No."

"So if all of the students are bored at various periods of the day, should they all fall down and roll around on the floor?"

"No."

"Should bored students be allowed to run butt-naked through the school, bring stereos, play basketball with the school trashcan, and practice fencing in class?"

"No."

"If I ever hear tell of you lying on the floor again, so help me, I'll send you to school in your pajamas and slippers with a written permission slip requesting an additional 30 minute nap for you like preschoolers. Do you understand?"

"Yes."

"What do you think you can do so that the class is not disrupted?"

"Maybe you could let me borrow some of your books in your library, and I could read."

At the tender age of 12, I wondered if he was ready for the harsh realities found in the biography world. That night I gave him Chris Gardner's biography, *"Pursuit of Happyness."* He read it in one day. While smiling and telling me how much he enjoyed reading it, he asked for another book. I handed him, *"A Child Called 'It'"* by David Pelzer. Within 24 hours he was ready for another. I handed him, *"A Piece of Cake,"* by Cupcake Brown, and many books began to follow. Desmond read so much, he began to fall asleep with open books in his lap, he slept on top of books and many nights I had to pry books out of his clutches as he slept with his face pressed against an open page.

After encouraging him to discuss the books, it became a ritual. By the end of the semester, he was reading college required literature, and teachers were writing home asking us to ban him from reading so much. Desmond's behavior issues were corrected, not by intensive therapy or various types of medications, but by stimulating his mind. I apologized to the teachers, but, one problem had been solved and I was not about to create another by taking the books away.

III. High School:
'You Don't Know Squat About Life At Sixteen'

Chapter 27

Mom: The New Anti-theft Device

"Good evening, may I speak to Ms. Chambers."
"Who's calling?" I indignantly asked, with my hand on my hip, and my eyes glued to the TV.

On this particular cool autumn night, the boys were attending separate sleepovers, LaCrystal was at the movies with a classmate, and Darrin had just arrived home with two DVD movie rentals from Blockbuster Video. He popped microwave popcorn, while I opened two Pepsi's, and got comfy under the comforter and waited for him. This was our once a month Friday night movie date, but as fate would have it, the phone rang. I got up, walked over to the telephone stand and answered it. I was emotionally fired-up and prepared to get hostile if it were telemarketers and bill collectors interrupting our limited time alone.

"Ms. Chambers, my name is Officer Adams of the Fredericksburg Sheriff's Department. I have your fourteen year old daughter, LaCrystal Smith, in my custody. She and a friend were caught stealing costume jewelry out of a store in the mall."

My brain began flip-flopping, asking and answering its own questions; How could she be at the mall, she's at the movies, right? This must be one of those radio station prank calls. But wait, I'm not even listening to the radio.

"What? I'm sorry, what did you say?" I asked.

"Ms. Chambers, we have your daughter and her friend on camera stealing costume jewelry. Your daughter acted as the "lookout" person while—"

"Is this a prank call?"

"No Ma'am. As I stated, we have your daughter in our custody right now. She had two pairs of earrings in her pocket. Her friend had several necklaces and pairs of earrings in each pocket."

The floor was beginning to sway and move closer to my face. I plopped down on the edge of the bed.

"Who is that?" Darrin asked, sitting up. "Who's that on the phone and what do they want?"

"Ma'am, because the value of the jewelry that your daughter stole is under $25.00, she can be charged with a misdemeanor—"

"Oh Lord," I interrupted with a loud moan.

"Give me the phone. Give me the damn phone." Darrin demanded as his voice began to rise and he attempted to pry the phone out of my hands. I yanked it back.

"Ma'am, most of the time kids do this to prove something. I had a private talk with your daughter, and she confided that she's never done anything like this. I could tell this stemmed from peer influence. Your daughter was very respectful, honest, and cooperative when arrested, unlike her friend. Ma'am, I would advise you to encourage your daughter to be more selective of her friends."

"Kelley, what is going on?" Darrin demanded again when he could not pry the phone from my grip.

I took one hand, covered the mouthpiece and told him that LaCrystal had been arrested for stealing earrings out of Hecht's Department store.

"What the—who the hell is that on the phone? I don't believe it." Darrin argued as he got out of bed.

"Shhh, it's a policeman. I'm sorry sir, what did you say?"

"I said, after talking with your daughter, the manager has decided not to press charges, but we'd like to know how soon you can come to the Hecht's security office and pick her up?"

"I can be there in ten minutes. Thank you very much Officer." I nervously said before hanging up. After slipping on my shoes and telling Darrin everything, I grabbed my purse and hurried out the door while he went into the bathroom to change. He was usually cool, calm, and reserved, that is until his baby girl ran into trouble, then he became an aggressive warrior.

"I'll call you if I need your help." I yelled while rushing out the front door and speed walking to the car. I slipped in a Liz McComb CD, rolled down the windows, and sobbed through the lyrics as I attempted to sing-along to the spiritual, *"Can't Nobody Know My Trouble but God."*

Arriving at the mall, I was directed to the security office. Standing on the outside of the door, I was unsure if I should knock hard and bold like the police or softly like the scared rabbit I was presently feeling like. I knocked softly and Officer Adams slipped into the hallway. He shut the door behind himself, and again, doted on how respectful and cooperative LaCrystal had been. After the pep-talk, he allowed me to enter.

Twelve TV monitors lined one wall as three security personnel glared at the screens, scanning various shoppers. LaCrystal sat in a chair next to a desk in the far corner. She kept her head down, looking at her folded hands. The infamous earrings sat on the desk beside her. They were the ugliest set of earrings I had ever seen. Picking up a pair and turning them over, I saw that they were $9.99 each. Why would she risk going to jail over these hideous, cheap things? I felt nauseous.

Something mentally clicked: This was an acceptance-theft. She did this to prove her loyalty to this girl. I turned to hear Darrin entering the security room with LaCrystal's jewelry box under his arm and her earring bag in his hand. He had taken it upon himself to drive to the department store and defend his daughter's honor. He calmly walked over and poured out the contents onto the desk. The bag held over thirty pairs of jumbled earrings, while the jewelry box stored countless necklaces, rings, and bracelets. I removed 14-kt gold earrings, diamond and opal birthstone earrings, jade earrings, genuine pearl studs, and spread them across the desk.

"Officer, I am so sorry, she—she didn't need to do this." I stammered and choked. Damn, I didn't want to start whimpering like a baby so I tried to control my emotions. LaCrystal continued to look at her hands in her lap.

"I know," he gently replied, "her friend, was rude and disrespectful and she had several necklaces and pairs of earrings in each pocket. The items totaled over $200.00. She could be charged with a felony. And ma'am, strictly off the records, she has been arrested before for theft. You really need to talk to your daughter about her friendship with this individual."

"Can I pay for the earrings?" Darrin interrupted, saving us from complete humiliation, as he gathered up the jewelry and quickly stuffed everything back into all the wrong compartments.

"Yes, you may take them to any register and pay for them." Officer Adams told him as he ushered us out of the office. I apologized again as LaCrystal and I headed for the car. Darrin told me that he would meet us at the house.

After a silent ride home, LaCrystal went to her bedroom. I tried to calm myself down before calling her into our bedroom and demanding her cell phone. She came and handed it to me and was about to turn and go back into her room when she stopped,

"Mom, I know you taught me better, and I want to do right, but when you're pressured by your friends, you forget everything your parents told you not to do." She quickly cried out. I placed the cellular phone on my end-table and sat quietly on the edge of the bed and listened, trying to think of what to say without causing the situation to escalate.

"LaCrystal, teenagers are supposed to have fun and hangout with their friends, but when you have to compromise your safety, steal, smoke drugs, get drunk, commit murder, sin, or allow your body to be used, it's time to stand back and reevaluate why you think this relationship is so important."

"But Mom, it's hard to make friends when kids just stare at you from head-to-toe and hate, for no reason. People aren't nice like they were in the olden days when you were young." She pleaded leaning against the door paneling.

"Has your friend ever stolen anything any other time when the two of you were together?"

"Yes, a shirt. She said she's able to save her weekly allowance from her father by stealing whatever she wants. And once she stole a cell phone from the teacher's drawer—but Mom, she didn't make me do it, honest, I wanted to see what it was like. She told me that sales people don't watch her because she's white and pretty."

I was beginning to feel sick again. Her classmate was not only a thief, but delusional was coming to mind.

"Have you stolen anything before?"

"Yes," she quietly answered and hung her head.

I held my breath as a lump crept up from my stomach and into my throat.

"What did you steal?"

"I watched out for my friend while she stole a cell phone from the teacher's desk drawer and then she looked-out for me while I stole ink."

"LaCrystal," I sighed, "I want you to know that when you're behind bars, sitting in a cemented cell, no one cares what color you are, how long your hair is, how pretty you are, or anything else about your personal features. You will become a state number. Your friend's father will probably bail her out of any situation she gets herself into, but I refuse to sit around and watch you throw your life away before it actually begins. I want you to decide if this girl's friendship is worth the headache and heartache she'll continue to bring."

"Mom, she's nice to me and she doesn't do the things most of the other girls do."

"Like what?"

"They go into the bathrooms and perform oral sex on different boys, and then they come back to school the next day bragging about it. They've been doing it since middle school. That's why most of them hate me, because I don't follow the crowd, but my friend isn't like that. She treats me like a friend and she's not a jealous person."

I sighed deeply. "What you're saying sickens me, and I don't know if teachers monitor the bathrooms like they should, but I promise you, I will make them aware Monday morning, and even though I can't determine what other parent's kids do, I can try my best to guide you. Sweetie, only sheep go to the slaughter-house without a fight."

She exhaled and looked away. This was going to have to be a hard lesson learned.

"I hear what you're saying, but that child's actions speak louder than her words. LaCrystal, don't allow anyone to jeopardize your future, in the name of friendship. You have the right to make choices, and that includes knowing that juvenile centers and jail should not be included on your resumé.

"Furthermore, from listening to that police officer, I knew this wasn't your friend's first time stealing or getting caught. She was too cocky and rude to be a rookie. And baby, she's not a true friend."

LaCrystal shifted, sighed uncomfortably again and crossed her legs as she leaned her back against the wall. She never spoke disrespectfully or attempted to rationalize her actions. But something in her eyes told me that my words were falling on deaf ears.

"I've always told each of you the truth, so has your Dad. We do that so all of you can learn from our mistakes and not make the same ones. The emotional and physical strain of being incarcerated and imprisoned can drive anyone insane. Before you were born, Darrin and I were both incarcerated.

"When those heavy iron cell doors close behind you, the only security you have is the folded jumpsuit you clutch tightly in your arms. As you're being led to your confinement, you realize no one can save you, not your mother, father, or your friends. When you have to stand face-to-face with a cell-mate that looks like a champion wrestler or maybe she could have formerly been a man, and she's looking at you like you are a chocolate bar and she's a kid in Willy Wonka's Chocolate Factory, no one has to tell you that your life is hanging on a wing and a prayer. Suddenly you can remember all those Sunday school prayers, because if you didn't believe before, you do now. But there is no one there to help you but Almighty God Himself.

"I have lived that life baby, so has your Dad. I had to fight for my food, my bed, telephone time, my womanhood and my life when I was incarcerated. I know what it's like to sleep cocooned like a newborn in hard, brittle, woolen horse-blankets. We both know what it's like to go to bed in fear and wake up in fear, to be afraid of being raped, shanked or labeled for showing emotional weakness and being caught off guard by a gang. We know what it's like to be at your lowest low and death seems to be a welcome gift."

LaCrystal lowered her head, clasped her hands, and played with her thumbs.

"Baby, I love you so much, that I'm willing to be tough and I'll risk you hating me for now, because I know you'll thank me in the years to come. I'm willing to sacrifice and even humiliate you and myself, if it keeps you out of jail, prison, off a street corner, off drugs, out of a coffin, and out of Satan's clutches. Your friend's lifestyle has a striking resemblance to that girl in the movie we watched, "*Thirteen.*"

She shifted from foot-to-foot then took a step further into our bedroom and leaned against the book-case sitting next to the door. She smoothed her tousled hair back and with far-away eyes, continued to half-listen. Tilting her head to the sound of Darrin coming in, I watched her body tense up. I knew she never wanted to let us down, especially her Dad.

Darrin carried a plastic grocery bag containing a Pepsi and a Ginger-ale. He walked past us, excused himself with a grunt, walked into the bathroom, and shut the door.

"Right now, as we speak," I continued, "that heifer is calling everyone, making sure the other kids know the details of you getting arrested. It's not a big deal for her, but to watch you sink like the *Titanic*, that's gossip for a bunch of high school kids."

We locked eyes. She looked at me with doubt, as if I were clueless to the wiles of this girl, as if this girl had more wisdom than her 40 year old mother of four, who had seen more than enough crap to fill a lifetime. I knew right then that LaCrystal's heart was in this friendship, and if I didn't snatch her from the mouth of the enemy, I could lose her, possibly forever. It was at that moment, I became willing to go out on a limb to save her.

"Oh, you don't believe me?" I asked as I reached for her cell phone, turned it on and handed it to her. There were eleven calls from classmates. Seven of the messages were from students that she said she never talked too, but, each person wanted to know the details of the theft and if they were really handcuffed and arrested. It was all a joke to a bunch of teenagers. She swallowed with shame and humility, and was sent to bed.

Darrin and I talked and cried until we fell into a restless sleep, only to wake up a few hours later and talked some more. We talked until the morning sun light fought its way through the tightly shut mini-blinds, forcing our heavy eyes to recognize a new day. I stumbled out of bed and began rummaging through my arts and crafts bin for supplies before going downstairs.

A short while later, I sat at the table with a hanging poster-board sign fit for a homecoming parade; complete with glitter, highlights, strings, and arrows pointing to the two pairs of hideous earrings, which were sealed in a Ziploc bag and stapled in the center of the sign. A little lower, spanning from side to side in bold black letters were the words: YESTERDAY, I WAS CAUGHT STEALING THESE EARRINGS FROM THIS STORE!

I went upstairs, entered LaCrystal's room, and woke her. She rolled over, blinked, and sat up.

"Wake up," I said as she fixed her swollen eyes on me. "Wash up and meet me downstairs."

Less than an hour later, she descended the stairs and walked towards the dining room table where I was sitting. When she saw the large neon green poster-board sandwich sign lying on the table, her eyes quickly filled with tears.

"We will be going back to the mall this morning for a few hours, so if you're hungry get a pastry strudel." I heard a crack in her voice as she held back emotions. "You will stand in front of the store wearing the sign for fifteen minute intervals, totaling two hours." I stood up and draped the poster over her chest like the "I AM A MAN" signs the Civil Rights Marchers wore in the 1960's. "I will be sitting in the car watching you the entire time."

She wiped away tears as we slowly walked out the front door to the car on that beautiful Saturday morning. It was 9:50 a.m.

We drove to the mall, in silence. I listened to our erratic breathing patterns; me inhaling, her exhaling, me inhaling, her exhaling. Pulling up to the entrance, I heard her catch her breath and we exited the car, she shuffled along behind me, with her head down. We found a spot near the entrance and after standing beside her for a few minutes, I walked back to the car, glancing over my left shoulder every now and then. I sat in the car, but never took my eyes off of her. Every fifteen minutes I got out and checked on her. If she needed to go to the bathroom, we went. If she wanted a drink, we went and got it. But we went back to that spot afterward.

Older adults stopped, read the sign, shook their heads and entered the store. Small children, held their parent's hands, and stared with mixed emotions. Teenagers stopped, gawked and nervously laughed, as they asked her questions and loudly thanked God it was not them.

After an hour, a frail, middle-aged woman approached LaCrystal and prayed with her. When the she left, I watched my daughter hold her head high and face her punishment with dignity. She never told me exactly what words were exchanged with the spiritually compassionate lady, but I did notice her entire demeanor change.

After two hours, we left the mall. As she entered the car and sat in the front seat, she leaned over, hugged and kissed me.

"Mom, you don't have to ever worry about me stealing again. I know it meant a lot to you to go through all these extremes just to teach me a lesson and keep me from going to jail."

We hugged again and cried and as I kissed her cheeks I reminded her that she deserved better than a permanent juvenile record. I reminded her that she was intelligent, responsible and beautiful and she could go to college and be anything that she wanted to be, but it depended on the choices she made right now. I told her that she deserved better than this, that she is better than this.

We went to lunch and enjoyed our day together. The earrings were donated to Goodwill and LaCrystal *never* stole again.

As for the friendship, it ended abruptly after a fight escalated over LaCrystal's refusal to lose her virginity at a mutual classmate's birthday sleepover. Her former-friend eventually spiraled out of control and before high school graduation, she was pregnant with her first child.

I did what I had to do to save my daughter that day. It was extreme, but readers, you already know that this book is about "extreme parenting." I'm not validating what I did, some may see it as cruel or wrong and some readers may wish they had done something similar to bring immediate changes in their teenager before they received permanent felony records. By the grace of God Almighty, my daughter avoided a juvenile record and was not arrested. I believe because of her character, respectful demeanor and humility, she was shown divine favor. I believe all of the talking and teachings and disciplinary methods actually worked in her favor this time.

This was my personal choice, not a method or guideline of teaching. Today, I watch my daughter's strength, character, sound choices and ability to overcome obstacles and persevere with a commitment and drive that is admirable.

Chapter 28

A Halloween Memory

I watched from my bedroom entrance as the boys noisily made their way up the stairs and blocked the hallway with Darrin's rickety work ladder.

"Let me go first Desmond, because I know where everything is." Travonté proclaimed loudly, as he pushed, shoved, and scrambled up the ladder and into the attic.

Desmond steadied the ladder and waited for Travonté to hand him the rectangular piece of drywall that served as an access panel. After placing the covering against the wall, he too, climbed up and into the attic.

"Hey," Travonté exclaimed. "How can I hand the stuff to you if you're up here with me—Ma, tell Desmond to get out of the attic."

"I can get my own costume," Desmond angrily shouted.

LaCrystal, who had been sitting on her bed listening to music, got up, squeezed past the ladder, rolled her eyes in annoyance at her brothers, and went into the hall bathroom.

"This is ridiculous. Desmond, you're just being difficult, Ma—"

"I don't want to hear that mess tonight or no one will be going trick or treating."

Silence emanated from the attic.

"Desmond, can you hold this while I look in those boxes?" Travonté asked, as he dropped something heavy in the attic above my head.

"Sure. There's a box over there in the corner marked

decorations, let's see what's in it." Desmond replied.

After nearly an hour, they crawled down the ladder with a large black trash bag and cardboard boxes marked "Halloween Items" and "Decorations."

"Travonté, please place the covering back up to the attic entrance, and put Dad's ladder outside."

After lugging the items down to the dining room and returning long enough to jam the access panel haphazardly back into place, spilling yellow insulation particles all over the hall, they bounded down the stairs with the ladder, banging it against every wall they came in contact with.

I went into my bathroom, opened the medicine cabinet and took out a bottle of Tylenol. After popping two 350 mg pills into my mouth, I turned on the faucet, placed my head under the spout, and filled my mouth with water. Standing upright, I closed my eyes, threw my head back, and swallowed. *This was going to be a long night.*

I opened my eyes and caught LaCrystal's reflection in the mirror.

"Aack" I yelled, "Sweetie, you scared me."

She was standing behind me, chuckling and shaking her head. "Mom, do you want to use your fog machine again? You still have a lot of unused fog juice left over from last year."

"I think that'll be a good idea." I replied as I listened to tearing sounds coming from the dining room as the boys began ripping the packing tape off of the boxes.

"LaCrystal, please go and see what they're doing, and while you're down there, find out if they got the fog machine out of the attic."

She descended the stairs, with her dog, Naomi, a miniature black Pomeranian, following closely behind dragging a red and black, stuffed ladybug in her mouth.

"Here's an eye patch and a parrot. I can go as a pirate," Travonté exclaimed, as he pulled various items out of the box, throwing them everywhere.

"I found your fireman's costume from last year," Desmond yelled back.

"Oh, you can go as a fireman this year Desmond." Travonté proudly proclaimed.

"I don't want to be a fireman. I want to—"

"Hey, what are ya'll doing?" Quasim asked, coming up the stairs, and stopping in the dining room. He had been watching TV in the family room when he heard all of the commotion. Peering into the boxes, he shook his head and laughed at them.

"We're getting out our costumes for tonight," they chimed.

LaCrystal stood over the boys and looked into the boxes. I came down the stairs and sat at the dining room table behind them.

"Travonté, hand me that black witch's hat," LaCrystal shouted, as he knelt over the box, with his head buried deep inside.

"Aren't ya'll a little too old to still be trick or treating?" Quasim said with a smirk on his face and laughed. "You're in middle school now."

"Quasim here's your last year's *Scream* mask," LaCrystal said, ignoring his snide comments and picking up the distorted, double-lined, plastic, skeletal face. She squeezed the button attached to a wire and watched as fake blood ran from the top of the skull, covered the face, and collected in the chin area, before being suctioned up and repeating the process again. She placed it on the table.

"Here's a black cape," Desmond shouted, as he reached in the box in front of him, pulled it out, and sat it on the floor.

"Quasim, that's yours from two years ago, remember when you went as Dracula?" LaCrystal reminded him, picking up the cape and placing it on the table next to the mask. Quasim looked at the cape and turned up his nose. Without acknowledging him, she reached over Desmond's head and exclaimed, "Mom, look, your witch shoe covers and those ugly, striped green stockings you wore last year." Pulling the items out of the box, she placed them on my lap.

"Ma, why don't you dress up and go with us?" Travonté asked, finally looking up from his box. "Nobody cares if you're old and you go trick or treating, as long as you have kids with you."

"Thank you Travonté, I will try my best to remember that."

"Mom, why don't we both go as witches? Here's your hat." LaCrystal said, handing me the extra-long, black hat.

"I'm not going as a fireman," Desmond reminded us, as he gathered the plastic fireman's jacket and helmet in his arms and put them back in the box.

"I'm going as Sean Taylor." Travonté proclaimed as he jumped up and ran down the stairs to their bedroom. "I'll wear my collector's jersey." His voice trailed from the basement.

"What can I go as?" Quasim muttered, while using his foot to separate the items already in a pile on the dining room floor.

"LaCrystal, here's Naomi's little devil costume," Desmond laughed and handed her the mini red body-cape with a spaded tail attached, and a horned head band. "Oh, and look, here's the fog machine and fog juice."

I don't have a costume," Quasim grumbled. He walked over to the black bag and turned it over, dumping the miscellaneous contents onto the floor. Vampire and jumbo crooked teeth, witch's noses and chins, matted afros, plastic knives, and other items fell out of the bag.

"Quasim, find something to mix and match," I encouraged him. "Learn to make do with what you have. That's what we're all doing."

"That's stupid."

"Whatever. You can put together a costume, wear last year's costume, or stay home and pass out candy."

Darrin entered the front door and Naomi ran up to him and

jumped up on his leg, greeting him with wet kisses. Patting her head, he loudly stated, "Nope. It's not happening. Handing out candy is my job. I've been doing it for years, and it's a big responsibility that I don't take lightly."

"Good evening," we all said as he entered the foyer.

"Good evening. Every Halloween me and Naomi hand out candy, and it ain't changing this year."

"I'll just wear last year's costume then," Quasim interrupted. He took the mask and cape off of the table and went downstairs.

As dusk moved in, changing a red-orange sunset to a deep blue, star-filled night, everyone ran up and down the stairs, yelling, grabbing and trading last minute costume details and pieces.

Darrin rushed into the shower, threw on lounge wear, and from under our bed he pulled out a secret stash of candy. Dumping M & M's, Snickers, Reese's Peanut Butter cups, and Hershey bars into a large orange bowl, he sat down on the edge of the bed, opened and crammed two Hershey's in his mouth, then turned on the TV to watch Halloween specials as he anxiously anticipated the doorbell.

Meanwhile, LaCrystal and I stood in my bathroom using spearmint gum adhesive to glue the bumpy noses and chins to our faces. I used paint to conceal my face and neck, and ended up with eerie hunter-green skin. LaCrystal, who was not able to use the paint because of skin allergies, put on the flesh colored pieces, which incidentally, matched her warm caramel complexion.

Afterward, she went to her room and returned dressed fashionably in black slacks, a fitting A-line black blazer, accented silver jewelry and carried a black plastic cauldron under her arm. She went downstairs, with Naomi sniffing and trailing behind. I followed after throwing on a black skirt, multi-colored top and long green press-on fingernails. Walking into the kitchen, I searched for grocery bags to hold candy.

Quasim came up behind me wearing his mask and vampire cape, which was too short, and much too tight around the neckline. He muffled a growl and flashed a rubber blade while pretending to stab me in the shoulder. Pushing the button on the mask, he caused the fake blood to flow.

Desmond and Travonté raced up the stairs, one behind the other. They were dressed in their favorite team's football jerseys. They wore heavy padding and equipment under the full uniform. Putting on their helmets, they strutted like peacocks in and out of the kitchen, enjoying the sound of their football cleats clicking on the ceramic tile floor.

I shook my head and laughed, while bending over to grab a handful of bags, flashlights and batteries from the kitchen junk drawer. LaCrystal sat on the stairs with Naomi snuggled in her lap. She quickly dressed her pet in the little red devil costume. Naomi was not too thrilled though. She jumped down, twisting her body to and fro, biting at the cape. Lowering her head, she rubbed her face along the dining room carpet in an attempt to remove the headpiece. After a few minutes of struggle and several dog treats from LaCrystal, she gave up. I must admit, she was quite adorable. The red costume highlighted her puffy black fur.

Travonté located the fog machine in his box. He filled it with fog juice, sat it beside the front door, and turned it on. Arranging my stereo behind it, he put in a Halloween scary sounds CD just as Darrin descended the stairs carrying his big bowl of treats, and an even bigger grin across his face.

Thick white fog filled the foyer and dining room area, as screams, creaking doors, and howls pierced the air. The special effects were awesome.

As we exited the front door, the mist led the way, forcing its way out onto the porch and down the stairs. Coming up the steps was a little princess, a Spiderman, an Ironman, and two Dora the Explorer characters.

Walking up the sidewalk, and feeling about as ridiculous as I could feel dressed in my witch get-up, I turned to see Darrin bending over and smiling like a kid at a carnival, as he ooh'd and aah'd over the costumes while handing out handfuls of assorted chocolates.

Trekking from house to house, we collected lots of candy. As their friends and classmates joined us, our group of five quickly became fifteen, including two additional preteens wearing vampire capes, and four teenagers wearing *Scream* masks.

Two hours later, with energy still running high, we walked past a dense thicket of trees. Someone in the front of the group pushed a branch out of his way and released it.

"Arrgh!" LaCrystal screamed, as a branch careened into her face, snatching off her chin, and hurling it into the woods. Everyone roared with laughter as we searched the woods in an attempt to find the chin. To this day, it was never located.

The kids begged me to walk with them to a few more houses in an adjacent neighborhood that supposedly gave out lots of candy. Reluctantly ignoring my aching feet, I agreed to walk them to the next location.

Hours later, returning home we passed the exact same thicket of trees. Someone in the front of the group pushed another branch out of his way and let it go.

"Arrgh!" LaCrystal screamed, with tears in her eyes. "That tree just snatched off my nose!" She felt around in the space where the nose had been glued on.

Everyone turned to see the spectacle and laughed until tears streamed from their eyes. After several minutes of searching, the nose, too, was lost forever. It was time to go home.

The porch light was off when we returned home because the unspoken Halloween rule is that porch lights off indicate the family is not participating with the Halloween activities, or they have no more candy. Our light out meant Darrin had given out all the treats.

Opening the front door, everyone ran into the living room, found an isolated spot, and dumped their bag of candy onto the carpet. They squealed over their findings and munched on monster eyes, ate Reese's Peanut-butter cups, and stuffed Bazooka Joe gum in their mouths as they separated unsealed and opened candy into a pile for trash, while placing their favorites and dislikes into two additional piles. As they excitedly shouted and traded Tootsie Roll Pops with Twizzlers, and Malted Milk Balls for Mini-Junior Mints and sticks of Laffy Taffy, I went upstairs to check on Darrin. I found him propped on pillows, snoring loudly in front of the TV, as Halloween specials blasted through the surround sound system. The empty orange bowl lay beside him. I smiled when I saw the pile of M & M's and Hershey bar wrappers crumpled beside him. This was indeed a memorable Halloween.

Chapter 29

"The roof, the roof, the roof is on fire"

"**M**om, Jared is having a party and we wanted to know if we could go?" Quasim asked, as he and his cousin DaVonté burst through the front door.

I continued to sit quietly at the dining room table reading Toni Morrison's, *Beloved*. I was engrossed in the good part, when Beloved comes out of the water and returns to Sethe the exact moment they bombarded my quiet time. Keeping my eyes on the book, I listened as they whispered back and forth.

I learned of Jared's unfavorable behavior through LaCrystal and her high school friends. The young man had been sexually active since middle school and at present, a high school classmate was pregnant with their first child. This was running through my mind when Quasim asked again.

"Mom, did you hear me?"

"Yes." I answered, slowly looking up at them. "Where is the party being held?"

"It's supposed to be at Jared's neighbor's house," Quasim stated as he leaned against the dining room wall partition. DaVonté casually stood nearby with his hands in his pockets.

"Why is it being held at his neighbor's house?"

"I don't know." Quasim replied, turning up his lip and rolling his eyes, as he nervously shifted from one foot to the other foot.

"How many chaperones will there be?" I asked, slowly placing the book flat on the table.

"Jared said there will be three chaperones." Quasim confidently stated and quickly glanced at DaVonté before returning his eyes toward me.

"Do you have a phone number for Jared so I can call and talk to an adult?"

"No. What do you need to do that for? I told you that they have enough chaperones."

"Son, I'd like to ask how many chaperones will be attending the party and their phone numbers. They may need help and I'd be happy to assist them."

Quasim let out a loud sigh and threw his hands up. "Well, I don't have anyone's number." He shouted.

"What time does the party start and when is it over?"

"I don't know. I guess when most teenagers' parties begin and end." He snapped.

That was not good enough for me. My b.s. antenna went up and was beeping rapidly, there was more to this story than what was being told. I sighed, sat up, and began removing the mint green, plastic hair rollers out of my hair. Both boys were silent as they watched me closely.

"Kelley, are you planning on going to the party as a chaperone?" DaVonté finally asked me with raised eyebrows.

"Heck no!" I quickly replied, "I'm going to get my party on since they don't need chaperones." I loudly shouted in a sing-song voice. Then I lifted my arms in the air and waved them from side-to-side while chanting, "The roof, the roof, the roof is on fire. We don't need no water—

"What? There is no way I'm going if she's going!" Quasim screamed, while pacing back and forth in the dining room like a caged leopard, mumbling something intelligible.

"LaCrystal," I yelled upstairs. "Please go into my bathroom and plug in my iron. Oh, and lay out my skinny jeans."

"Are you serious?" Quasim screeched. "This is crazy. This is torture. What type of *"old"* parent goes to a teenager's party?"

"A parent that wants to protect their 14-year old child, that's what type of *"old"* parent goes to a teenager's party."

"This is ridiculous." Quasim shouted. He threw his hands up in the air in an act of surrender. "You are ridiculous. I won't go. Forget it. I'll stay home before I go to a party with you."

I picked up my book, yelled upstairs for LaCrystal to unplug the iron, and smiled to myself as Quasim and DaVonté went downstairs to the family room to play video games. Mission accomplished.

Chapter 30

Do Your Pants Hang Low?

When the sock trolls vacated the premises, the belt trolls moved in, and possibly stole all of Qausim's belts.

Each week, his pants began hanging lower and lower, and each week, we saw more and more of his underwear and butt imprints. The pants went from oversized and baggy, to peek-a-boo boxers, to boxers and bun-cheeks, and finally ended on his upper thighs.

Personally, I preferred not to see the curvature of his butt, nor his paisley blue boxers. Whenever asked to pull up his pant, he would snatch them up to his chest and yell, "Is this what you want, for me to look like a freakin' nerd?"

We argued daily over the choice of how he wore his clothes. On occasion, I attempted to grab his jeans and pull them up whenever his underwear and butt imprints were revealed.

After receiving several frustrated calls and emails from his teachers and the high school principal, one evening I decided to call him into the kitchen for a heart-to-heart conversation.

"Quasim, please go into the powder room and for ten minutes, look at yourself in the mirror from head to toe, then come back and explain to me the significance of your fashion statement."

He rolled his eyes, sucked his teeth, turned and with legs wide open, stomped out of the kitchen.

Snatching the powder room door open he went in, only to return to the kitchen a few seconds later and leaned against the dishwasher. Crossing his arms, he impatiently waited, ready to blow-up at any minute.

"Son, your teachers have a problem with the way you're wearing your pants," I said as I leaned against the opposite counter and faced him.

"So, everybody wear their pants low. It's stupid to wear them jacked-up."

Have you looked at the bottom of your jeans? Why do you think they look like you pulled them out of a shredder?"

"They drag because they're too big." He stated with a matter of fact arrogance.

"Should we make sure your jeans are smaller?"

"No. This is the style. Did my teachers tell you if they were calling everyone's parents?"

"I don't know and I don't care. You are my concern."

He rolled his eyes.

"This isn't a private school. How we dress shouldn't matter. Those teachers need to focus on our grades, or what some of those students are doing in the bathrooms." He argued and looked to the ceiling.

"Would you be fine with your male teachers walking up and down the aisle with their pants hanging down and showing their butt-cheeks, or what if your female teachers came in showing their pink frilly bloomers? Would that be respectful?

"No, that would be gross and stupid."

"Well son, what makes you think everyone wants to see you and your friends' underwear?"

Without answering, he released an impatient sigh and looked away.

"Do you know where this ridiculous fashion craze came from?"

"No."

"It started in California, in prisons by gay male inmates. In the late 1980's the prisoners wore their pants low to show their butt in an attempt to arouse other male inmates in hopes of gaining sexual encounters. It's similar to the expressions prostitutes use when they dress provocatively to draw in men. Quasim, are you sure you want to emulate gay prisoners?"

Silence, as he pondered my question. I knew at that point, I had to keep his attention or within seconds, it could be lost forever.

"You're turning sixteen, and soon you'll be out looking for a job. Do you think clothing stores and restaurants will hire you or any of your friends, with your pants hanging down to your thighs? No." I answered my own question. "No one will hire any teen that comes strolling in their establishment looking like a thug or a gangster-rapper. But they will call the police on you. Son, you can't become a respectful citizen when you're doing everything possible to make yourself a menace to society."

Silence.

"Quasim, you are better than this. You have the chance to grow up and be anything that you want to be. You don't have to settle for the types of jobs Black Americans had to accept before, during and after the Civil Rights Era. Son, God has bigger plans for your life other than being an unemployed thug. You don't have to follow every fashion craze that hits the streets. You don't have to try every drug, drink everything offered at parties, or sleep around because everyone else is doing it. If you really want popularity and friends that look up to you, it doesn't come with following everything they do, it starts with being different and standing out from the crowd. Before the conductor can lead an orchestra, he must first turn his back on the crowd. Don't you get it? You have to step away from the crowd to become a leader. We're trying to raise strong rams, not sheep that are afraid to step out of the herd. If you want to be a follower, then follow the Lord. I promise you, He won't lead you astray.

"The way you dress and carry yourself plays a major role in

who you'll encounter in life, and where you'll end up. Think about if you were sick and went to a doctor, and he entered the examining room wearing a jersey, a baseball cap turned to the side, and his jeans hanging down showing his underwear, and he was rapping to Tupac, I don't think you'd be so accepting of his credentials. I believe you'd get out of that office so fast you'd leave a trail of smoke, especially when he opens his mouth and asks, "What up dawg?"

Quasim looked at me like I had lost my mind, and even though he did not say a word, somehow, I knew exactly what he was thinking: *Why would someone with a good job and a nice career, dress and act so foolishly?*

"Exactly son," I exclaimed rather loudly. "It's immature and maturity begins right now, when you act as a responsible teenager."

His head jerked in my direction and his wide startled eyes were my confirmations. "Every day we make a choice to either follow the world's ways or we can take a stand as individuals and walk our own paths, setting our own trends."

"But I'm just a kid right now. I don't want to think about life stuff. I just want to have fun." He said, shifting his body and crossing his legs as he continued to lean against the dishwasher. "And anyway, I like the way I dress. No one tells you how to dress."

This heart-to-heart was about to get ugly, and I had no intentions of battling with a fifteen year old.

"Son, while you're doing everything you can to impress your friends—"

"I'm not trying to impress anybody," he interrupted, "I just like to dress the way I want to. It's not hurting anyone."

"While you're trying to dress like a thug to impress your friends," I continued, "we already know that it's only a matter of time before your attire attracts the wrong type of friends, and then they'll begin to influence your attitudes and eventually your actions. In the meantime, I can promise you one thing, Dad and I will not contribute to your wardrobe expenses as long as you're damaging your character. We won't pay for you to look like a gangster or a thug."

"So, I'll just get a job and buy my own clothes. I don't ask y'all for nothing anyway."

"Correction, every day that you play video games and watch football all weekend, you're relying on us to keep the electric running. Every time you eat an entire box of Froot Loops and a gallon of milk in one sitting, you're relying on us to provide food to fill your belly. And when I miss work because I have to sit in the principal's office trying to get you back in school, after yet another suspension, and I don't get paid when I'm off from work, you're relying on us. And just so you know, I've been studying the Bible in an attempt to learn how to forgive and love difficult people like Jesus did, but I'm not there yet. I still have some sinner's traits, I'm a work in progress, trying to get it right. So I'm advising you to show some respect and control the venom on your tongue. Don't dig your own grave, you might slip and fall into it or get pushed."

"I respect you," he shouted, "but that doesn't have anything to do with how I dress."

Closing the discussion, which was about to escalate, I reminded him. "Son, I am asking you for the last time to pull up your pants and stop showing your underwear. It's trifling, inappropriate and disgusting."

I turned, and with my back to him, began yanking out seasonings, flour, and Crisco to fry chicken for dinner. Quasim shuffled around behind me for a few seconds before blurting out, "Are you done?"

"Yes." I answered without turning around.

He left the kitchen to go downstairs to the family room. I cringed when I glanced and saw four to five inches of red boxers and his jiggling butt imprints. Unbeknownst to either of

Damn the Nanny 145

us, over the next few months, everything, including my sanity, would be put to the test because of his choices.

As days turned into weeks, and weeks into months, Quasim's behavior spiraled out of control. His "rapper" persona increased, and he began to lash out at all authoritative figures and refused all clinical counseling when I suggested it.

After school, on sunny warm days, he and his friends, all with their pants hanging down to their thighs, gathered on our porch and performed free-style rap songs. We had to step over and maneuver our way through them, as they refused to get up and allow us entrance into our own home. Eventually, Darrin began asking Quasim to keep his friends off of the porch, so whenever our car entered the parking area, the young men would disperse, but always returned in a day or two.

One morning, during this tumultuous rebellious period, the high school principal called and described in detail that Quasim had earned a three-day suspension for using explicit rap lyrics in class and when reprimanded by the teacher, I was told he retaliated, by shouting inappropriate obscenities. I was filled with rage because I knew the teacher would not lie on him. This was extreme disrespect and no one deserved this type of treatment.

Later that night, Darrin and I sat at the dining room table for two hours, which denied everyone else homework assistance, and had a heated back-and-forth discussion with Quasim. He denied everything and refused to accept responsibility for his destructive behavior. He claimed the teacher lied on him.

I issued a one-day "suit punishment" upon returning to school and no phone privileges for a week. Quasim went ballistic. He felt the punishments were ridiculous and too harsh. The situation intensified when he threatened to run-away rather than wear the suit. We watched as he grabbed a black trash bag, ran downstairs, filled it with a handful of shoes and clothes, and came up the stairs. As he stomped out the front door, I was already on the phone calling the police.

In minutes they arrived and met Quasim as he walked up the sidewalk. He was escorted back home and stood in the front yard talking with an officer. Darrin and I stepped out on the porch, waiting our turn. The officer listened to Quasim's tirade over the unfairness of his punishment.

After listening patiently, the officer explained to Quasim the benefits of respecting his teachers and his parents. Quasim rolled his eyes, hummed, and sucked his teeth as the officer spoke with genuine concern. He told Quasim that there were thousands of teenagers behind bars with the same type of "go-hard, thug-life mentality," and he warned that he would see Quasim again, soon, if he did not change his attitude.

After relating our version of the incident, and spending an additional hour ignoring Quasim as he acted out disrespectfully to us and the officer, we walked into the house mentally exhausted, Quasim followed. Our son was out of control.

I began to snoop, ask questions, read body language, and when necessary, I began to sniff for unknown odors. Drugs and alcohol or drugs did not seem to play a role in his behavior, but, Quasim continued to glamorize the celebrity rapper's lyrics, their fashion style, and their lifestyles, all his focus was on becoming a famous rapper.

I prayed for an end to this rebellious spirit, and I prayed for myself, because my patience was running low. At this point Darrin was beginning to pull away. He was becoming more and more withdrawn, distant and moody with me and the family, and he was staying at work for longer hours, more days and more emergencies.

While shampooing the dining room carpet one Saturday afternoon, I put on an Otis Redding CD and began singing and gently swaying to *Sitting on the Dock of the Bay* as I slowly pushed the Bissell back and forth.

Quasim was listening to his iPod when he came up the

stairs. He looked at me with a defiant smirk, stretched his legs wide with each step to keep his jeans from falling down to his knees, and casually walked through the dining room.

"Quasim, you need to pull up your jeans."

He continued walking toward the front door.

"Quasim," I repeated, "pull up your jeans."

He sucked his teeth, kept walking and grumbled, "Man, fuck this shit."

I snapped. Yes readers, temporary insanity. All sense of rationale, logic, positive reinforcement, and all that other stuff you read in those parenting books didn't mean diddley. It went out the window.

Some readers may never publically admit that once or twice, when a confrontation arose with their defiant teenager, they may have lost their composure. I am willing to acknowledge that my cup had runneth over.

Standing there with my mouth opened wide enough to catch flying ping pong balls, I stood in shock as he slammed the front door behind himself.

I knew that this was what the teachers were experiencing and as thoughts of my ancestors who were murdered to give him the opportunity to attend public school ran through my mind. I thought of how all of their struggles did not mean squat to him and his generation. Quasim's privileged and entitled attitude combined with his wanna-be hard, disrespectful gangster mentality had me so angry I saw stars appear before my eyes.

I took deep breaths and looked down at my hands, which were trembling so badly it was hard for me to hold onto the handle of the Bissell. Hell, I forgot the machine was even running.

In seconds, I saw myself getting closer and closer to Quasim. I was coming up behind him as he walked up the sidewalk bobbing his head up and down to the musical beats coming from his iPod. It was as if I were standing on *The Jetson's* fast moving sidewalk, when I heard someone shout, "If you don't want to wear the damn pants, take them off!" It was moments before I realized the shout came from me.

Numerous red and brown rubber-bands twisted around the boxer shorts sprang up in the air and went flying in every direction. A fat beige one hit me on the forehead as Quasim yelled and clutched at the extra-extra-large boxers in an attempt to keep them from falling down.

One hand held onto the boxers while the other waved back and forth in an attempt to catch the somersaulting iPod that gravity was clearly claiming.

It hit the ground and broke apart.

"What the—Here! Take the stupid pants." He shrieked. Sliding out of his untied Jordan basketball shoes, then stepping out of his jeans. He kicked them to a nearby patch of grass.

As he held onto the boxers with a balled fist, he raised the other hand in the air like Napoleon going into battle and with the iPod cord dangling around his wrist, he shouted, "If I have to wear them like a freakin' nerd, then I won't wear them at all!"

"Whatever, you weren't trying to actually wear them anyway." I shouted back while walking over to the jeans, snatching them up and stuffing them under my arm, walking back down the sidewalk, I sang:

"Do your pants hang low? Do they wobble to and fro?
Can you tie them in a knot? Can you tie them in a bow? Can you keep them up with a belt, like a Continental Soldier? Do your pants hang low?"

Quasim followed me in t-shirt, boxers, socks, and shoes.

"Dad told me that someone was taking his socks and underwear. How did you get his boxers?" I asked, placing his jeans on the kitchen counter.

"They were mixed in my clothes." He answered.

"He doesn't wash his clothes with yours, so how are they getting mixed in?"

"I don't know, they just did," He calmly stated.

"Well, the next time his socks or underwear magically ends up with yours, try giving them back to him."

I walked into the dining room, looked at the Bissell, which was still running, and started shampooing again. Quasim went down to his room.

Several minutes later, he came bouncing up the stairs completely dressed. Passing through the dining room, he jerked up his shirt, smiled, and showed me that his jeans were being held up on his waist by a belt, and none of his underwear was showing.

"Son, thank you very much, you look nice." I said with a smile. I walked over, hugged him, and gave him a peck on the cheek.

"You're welcome." He said as he smiled and went out the front door, quietly shutting it behind him.

With this battle over, I wondered what the next one would be as I leaned over the Bissell. Closing my eyes, I bowed my head and thanked the Lord for allowing my son to keep me on my knees in prayer. I prayed for strength, an ounce of wisdom and patience to endure anything else that would be placed in our path. I thanked Him for allowing that confrontation to end peacefully.

Chapter 31
My Name Ain't Clara Belle

I listened quietly as the principal explained me that Desmond had been drawing and passing out sexually graphic and explicit materials during class. The illustrations had earned him a one day suspension. Hanging up the phone, I exhaled loudly while rubbing my throbbing temples then called Darrin.

After school, Desmond walked in the front door with his head hanging down. I stood in the kitchen opening and closing the refrigerator, then the freezer section, trying to decide what to prepare for dinner. He sat his book bag on the kitchen floor and sat on a stool. I walked over to the junk drawer and took out pencil and paper, then placed them in front of him.

"Son, please draw me a copy of what you drew in school."

He dropped his head lower and pouted. I placed five bell peppers in the sink and began slowly washing them. After more than ten minutes Desmond still had not drawn anything.

"Sweetie, do you need help getting started?" I asked with an intentional extra amount of concern in my voice.

"No thank you."

"Exactly what were you were trying to draw?" I asked as I peered over his shoulder pretending to grab a spatula from the utensil rack.

"It was just stupid breasts."

"Well by golly," I exclaimed, "I know I can help you with that, I happen to own not one but two of them."

As tears formed in his eyes, I gently touched his shoulder.

"Oh son, don't cry," I cooed, "I take great pride in helping you. I didn't know when you would be ready for "the talk." If you're interested in the woman's body, or if you like drawing breasts, then I intend to make sure they're the best Caravaggio like pieces in Fredericksburg, Virginia. I want to make sure they're as close to Da Vinci looking breasts as possible."

"Don't you see, that's the problem," he angrily shouted. "You take the fun out of stuff. You always have to use logic. Then it's not funny anymore. Everything has to be a learning experience with you. We can't do anything sneaky, wrong, or bad and just get away with it like other kids. Our friend's parents just turn their heads and pretend they didn't see their kids doing bad stuff because they love them. But not you, noooo, you have to call us on everything and make us learn something from it. That's not right."

"Aw, thank you sweetie," I beamed. "I'll take that—"

"See," he groaned. "You're doing it again! Why can't you be like normal parents? Why can't you just beat us and get it over with. Why do you have to drive us nuts with your lectures and punishments?"

"Desmond," I said with seriousness, "I am sure you already know that your mother is not like anyone else's. I don't compare you with other people's kids, so don't compare me with other people's parents. Yes, I don't condone a lot of things some parents accept. Some parents allow their children to smoke weed and drink at home, I don't. Some parents allow their teenagers to have overnight guests of the opposite sex, I'm not. And some parents make excuses for their teenager's behavior, I don't.

"I don't want any of you to be the school's jester. You're all too intelligent and you have too much potential for me to accept this type of foolishness."

"You're always saying that we're too smart, we're too handsome, and we're too gifted to act foolishly, but only you think that. What if we don't think that about ourselves?" He complained then released a sigh and looked at me before lowering his head.

"Desmond, you have more potential than you can imagine, and my job is to help you see that. You don't have to walk around blind-folded or play the stupid class clown to be liked. All of you have unimaginable opportunities at your fingertips. You just have to be willing to make the right choices now so that the doors aren't shut in your face later.

"As for the drawings, everything that God made on the woman's body was put there for a reason, and He perfected man the same way, so both of our bodies deserve respect."

He kept his head lowered as he painstakingly drew two long, droopy, pear shaped, water balloon characters. I gasped as I looked at the ridiculous things.

"Boy, my name ain't Clara Belle the Cow, and I definitely don't look like that. No human female looks like that. Those are eight inch udders."

He attempted to conceal the drawing with his hands as he tried to erase and correctly draw what he believed the female nipple resembled.

Meanwhile, I went upstairs to our home library, pulled out my old college health education book and returned to the kitchen. Placing the book in front of him, I flipped to the human body and reproductive section. Sitting down beside him, we studied the illustrations and correct terminology. He was apprehensive at first, but as he saw that I was being honest with him, he warmed up and began to ask detailed questions.

Darrin arrived home from work a little while later and came into the kitchen. He looked at the picture, then to Desmond, then to the open health book. He shook his head.

"Son, you're getting too old for this type of foolishness," he said, "I bet after this learning session you won't be so quick to ridicule any parts of anybody's body."

Leaning against the kitchen counter, Darrin crossed his arms and we began openly discussing health education; the human body, sex, sexually transmitted diseases, childbearing and anything else that Desmond questioned us about. We eventually addressed the credibility of street knowledge and what he may have heard from his friends, compared to what is actually happening to the human body.

Later that night we challenged Desmond to go back to school, after his suspension, and encourage his friends with truth. We told him to watch their reactions. He agreed and followed through.

When he came home though, he had a completely different perspective. It's funny how truth isn't as hilarious as ignorance. That was the last time he ever ridiculed the human body.

Chapter 32

Free Tutoring

"Do we have to go over this every week?" I asked Quasim. "I know high school can be distracting but you're in 9th grade now Quasim, every final grade you receive on your report card determines where you will go after graduation, and we all know you can do better than this." I said while looking at all of the missed assignments, failed quizzes and tests, and low grades on his interim report.

"I have three more years to bring my grades up." He nonchalantly replied.

"Y'all told us that you wanted to earn extra money," I said, including LaCrystal, Travonté and Desmond in the conversation, as they hung out in the kitchen listening, "And we're willing to give allowances for keeping your grades and your grade point averages up, but we're not going to pay any of you to fail."

After dinner they usually hung around in the kitchen and talked about sports, the events of the day, or the latest happenings at school. On this particular day, as they washed dishes and laughed and talked, Quasim sat beside me at the dining room table, waiting quietly while I read his interim.

It pained me to see numerous F's and D's on the small pink wrinkled paper that showed his weekly performance. I knew Darrin and I had tried everything possible to encourage, assist and help all of them make passing grades and do well in school. The television was not turned on during study time, the cell phones were blocked, and everyone was required to use light conversation while others studied.

Everyday Darrin and I asked each of our children if they had any homework assignments, upcoming quizzes, or tests. We would then assist them for an hour. Only afterward would we retreat upstairs and attempt to relax. But, if one child did not cooperate with the homework system, everyone paid the price.

Quasim, being his usual self, would put us to the test. Each week he told us that he had everything under control. Unfortunately, when we received the semester interim report, and it was lined with missing homework, failed quizzes and low tests, we knew that nothing was really under control except his social life.

Normal disciplinary methods did not work with this son. If we took away his phone privileges, he borrowed someone else's. When he was put on punishment, he broke it or disregarded it, as he continuously found ways to undermine all authority. Darrin and I knew Quasim was a bright student, but he was determined to express academic laziness, stubbornness, and rebellion. Trying to discuss his grades nearly always turned into a heated confrontation. It was time for extreme psychological parenting to get his attention and hopefully turn this declining lack of enthusiasm for his education around.

"Beginning today, I will personally tutor anyone failing. Having a 'D' or 'F' average is considered failing." I explained.

"Why are you worrying about my grades?" Quasim angrily blurted out. "If I fail it's my business, not yours. This is my life, why can't I live it like I want to?"

"All of you have been medically tested," I loudly stated, talking to no one in particular, all the while ignoring Quasim's ranting and raving, "And we know that none of you have learning, mental, or physical disabilities, or any other type of psychological disorders that would interfere with your learning capabilities. You are old enough to comprehend your assignments, and you're capable of studying. You get regular eye exams, so I know you can see the board and read what is written. We do our job as parents, and we expect you to hold your end of the bargain by doing your job as students.

I got up and walked into the kitchen. Going to the refrigerator, I took out two celery stalks. After slicing them into several slits and adding squeeze cheese and garlic powder, I poured a glass of prune juice and took the snacks to the dining room.

I knew I had to reach Quasim on an entirely different plateau, and I was willing to go there. It was my intention to make this experience so intolerable it would encourage him to take immediate accountability for his own homework and study habits. Saying a silent prayer that this plan worked, I sat down beside him.

With a celery stick hanging out of the side of my lips like a dangling pipe, I scoot my chair next to his. He rolled his eyes then grabbed the sides of his chair, and with his body, hopped his chair a few inches away from mine. Each time I moved closer to him, he hopped further away. Out of the corner of my eye, I could see him warily peeking at me. Let the games begin!

"Well son, why don't we get started." I said, blowing an excessive amount of air toward him as I pronounced each "w" with exaggerated winded effects. The celery, cheese and garlic smell lingered in the air.

"What subject will be first?"

He leaned away from me as he pulled out his science book, trying to avoid all contact with my breath.

"Well let's go. Let's get to work, work, work," I cheered as I clapped my hands enthusiastically like the Clumps at the dinner table in *The Nutty Professor*. "I love science."

He slouched down about an inch in his chair and clutched the science book. I pried the book out of his fingers and slid it toward me.

"Wow, we're discussing the weather?" I asked with a broad

smile, talking directly into his face, while crunching loudly on another piece of celery.

"Can you please turn your head that way when you talk?" He asked, pointing his index finger in the opposite direction.

"Sure." I said. Turning away for a few seconds, I picked up my glass, gulped some prune juice and let out a loud lingering, prize-winning, country fair belch. Covering my mouth like a bashful, genteel lady, I finished with a hiccup. Fanning my mouth lightly while excusing myself, I smiled with sincerity as I turned back toward Quasim.

If he could have given birth to two calves, a kitten and a hamster at that moment, he probably would have. His facial expression of shock, disgust and disbelief was a priceless Kodak moment.

"I can do it myself." He yelled, sliding his book away from me. "I don't need any help."

"Son, your interim says different. It's says you need lots of additional help." I cooed while sliding the book back to me. "And guess what, you don't even have to pay me, I'll tutor you every day for free."

"Oh no you won't, I can do it myself." He pleaded and attempted to pull the book out of my grip.

"Quasim," I said seriously, "I can sit here every night and tutor you or I can allow you to complete your own homework assignments and study for tests without me standing over you like a prison warden. The choice is yours. Do I have to sit down and tutor you?"

"No, never again, I promise."

"Do you plan to bring those grades up in the next three weeks before the grading period ends?"

"Yes, I can do it." He eagerly replied.

"I'm going online, and I'll check your progress."

"Okay." He quickly answered. He buried his face in the science book and began looking up his assigned definitions.

I got up, rubbed his hair in approval on my way to the kitchen, walked over to the sink, poured out the prune juice and took the celery upstairs with me to munch on. I never had to tutor him again, and Quasim's grades never went below a passing "C" average.

He became determined to make sure he graduated on time. I reminded all of our teenagers regularly that they did not have to pay rent. I did not expect them to work and pay bills. I did expect them to try to keep their grades up and graduate from high school. I did expect them to attend some type of college, trade school, or join a branch of the military after graduation. They would not be allowed to graduate, work at a local restaurant and live off of their parents. To give them an idea of the real world, I told them that if they did not attend college, which was the best plan for all of them, but instead they choose to stay within the area and work, they would have to sign a lease with us and pay their own cell phone bill and rent. The rent would be a mandatory $500.00 a month. If they chose to go to college, we would provide free phone service, meals and transportation (a used car).

I made sure they knew that there would be no dropping out of school, staying out all night and sleeping all day. I reminded them that local restaurants did not pay enough for what I demanded as rent, so their best choice was to go to college or go into the military. I did not condone jail, sleeping on the couch all day, or bringing home two bags of greasy French-fries and old burgers and expecting that to suffice as a contribution to the house-hold expenses. Nope. They had to do better than that.

For years I had each of them tested for mental, emotional, physical, psychological and social deficiencies, they were all healthy, happy, smart-aleck growing teens, so I would treat them accordingly.

I looked forward to the years of the "Empty Nest" and retirement. I even cringed with the thought of our grandchildren coming to visit and they come running to us crying because they cannot watch cartoons because their 30 year old Uncle So-and-So is sprawled out on the couch playing video games, eating cheese puffs and drinking Pepsi. Nope, it's not happening.

Chapter 33

Boomerang Phone

Desmond startled me as I turned around to look in one of the kitchen cabinets for a large bowl to make brownies.

"What's the problem sweetie?" I asked as I watched his body slump down onto a stool.

He gave a loud sigh, shifted and slumped lower. I could tell by his movements that this was a big one and it had been bothering him for a while.

"What's troubling you?" I asked, turning down the music playing from my stereo and facing him. "What is it Desmond? If something is bothering you, then it's bothering me, so what's bothering us?"

"I miss the school bus every morning, so I miss breakfast, and then I have to starve until lunch."

"Son, what time are you getting up?"

"I set my alarm but I never hear it go off."

"Why can't you hear your alarm clock go off?"

"Because I'm too tired to hear it so I sleep right through the buzzing."

"Why are you so tired every morning that you sleep through the buzzing?"

"Because I can't sleep at night."

"And why is it that you can't sleep at night?" I asked him, knowing he wanted me to pull it out of him. He let out another loud sigh and rotated on the stool. This was almost like going through an obstacle course. I had to go through the maze, jump through fire, and perform death defying acts just for him to open up and tell me what was bothering him.

"Would you like for me to start waking you up in the morning when I get up?"

"No."

"Would you like to go to bed earlier?"

"No."

"Are you ready to tell me why are you so tired every morning?"

"Because of Quasim." He blurted out angrily.

Ding, ding, ding. I had asked the magical question. Now how his lack of sleep related to Quasim was the next million dollar question would I have to resort back to the obstacle course again?

"Desmond, please explain to me how Quasim makes you tired in the morning?"

He dropped his head into his hands and said, "He talks to girls on the phone all night until one or two in the morning, and if he's not on the phone, he lies in bed 'rapping' all night."

"Would you like to take a nap until dinner is ready?"

"Yes."

He got off the stool and headed downstairs to take a nap. I stood in the kitchen thinking of how I would confront Quasim.

"Thank you for telling me what was bothering you," I yelled after Desmond as he closed his bedroom door.

We played a family game of Scrabble before bedtime, but, before crawling into bed, I set my alarm clock to wake me at one o'clock in the morning.

Darrin stirred when the alarm sounded, mumbled something incoherent, and quickly drifted back into a deep sleep. I got up, said a mental prayer that Quasim would prove me wrong and picked up the house phone. I could hear him attempting to disguise his voice and speak in this deep masculine and supposedly sexy tone then laughed as the young lady giggled and cooed on the other end. I felt nauseous.

"Boy, have you lost your mind?"

"I'm on the phone." He snapped.

Now Quasim knew he was wrong and he knew the gig was up, but what really choked me up was how he had the audacity to tell me to hang up the phone that I pay for, so he could continue his conversation on a school night.

I slammed the phone down, put on my robe, and marched down the stairs. I went to his bedroom, opened the door and saw him sprawled across his bed laughing and continuing his conversation.

"Quasim, unplug the damn phone and bring it upstairs right now."

"Can I get up?" He said with an attitude. "I'll bring it when I get up."

"Now!" I said, turning away and shutting the door behind me. I began mentally counting sheep, boots, buttons and the spiders flying away out of Charlotte's Web and anything else that popped into my head to keep my mind off of strangling that boy.

As I reached the top level leading to our bedroom, Quasim swung the door open and yelled, "Here!"

"Upstairs. Now!" I shouted.

He stomped out of his bedroom and up the stairs behind me, grumbling and complaining the entire way.

"Here!" He yelled when he reached me and threw the phone.

By sheer reflex, I turned and caught the base as it made contact with my chest. The handle piece hit my elbow as I raised my arm to protect my face. Yeah, he had finally lost his everlasting mind. This is how I know I needed the Lord's presence in my life. If I had to compare my son to any Biblical person, he would be compared to Judah, Jacob's son, the rebellious warrior and fighter. Always ready to battle.

His facial expression showed recognition that he realized he had just crossed the line as he turned and tried to run back down the stairs. I squeezed the base of the phone in one hand and threw the connected receiver piece. Somehow, the receiver's coil had wrapped itself around my wrist. As I hurled it, the phone miraculously followed him down the winding staircase as he was skipping every other step, in a futile attempt to put distance between us. I watched as the receiver traveled at an accelerated speed and found its mark. "Thock!"

"Ouch," he yelled, grabbing the back of his head.

Like a boomerang, the receiver recoiled and came back to me, landing at my feet. I leaned over, picked it up, and went into my room. I could hear Quasim calling me crazy, and threatening that he would get his own phone because he wasn't putting up with my mess anymore. I shut my bedroom door and went back to bed. I never put another phone in their bedroom. The house phone was put in the kitchen and if anyone wanted to use it, they had to sit in the kitchen, which put brakes on privacy because as you know, I love cooking, so I was always in the kitchen listening.

Quasim grew tired of hiding his mouth with concealed hands as he whispered lies to the females, but there were no more negotiations, and he never threw anything else at me either.

Chapter 34

Las Vegas Slots

"Mom, my friend's having a sleepover, can I go?" Quasim yelled up from the bottom of the stairs one windy fall Friday night.

Closing my Bible, I looked at the clock and an intense feeling of dread and discord came over me. My stomach flip-flopped and I took a few deep breaths. It was a little after nine and Darrin lay next to me snoring, snorting and coughing every few minutes.

"Sure," I answered, "as long as I have spoken to his parents about the arrangements."

"What do you mean the arrangements?"

Standing up, I laid the Bible on the bed and went to the top of the stairs.

"You know," I slowly said looking down at him, "Stuff like, who will be chaperoning the teenagers? What is the itinerary for the night? When are you to return home? Who else will be spending the night? You know, just all of that nosey parent type of stuff?"

"Why are you the only parent who feels you have to know everything, other parents don't do all this mess?"

"Either I talk to his parents or you don't go. Period!" I went back to my room, picked up the Bible and attempted to finish reading *Isaiah 53*, NIV but my concentration was completely gone.

"Man, I hate this place." Quasim shouted and stomped to his room, slamming the door behind him.

An hour later he came back to the bottom of the stairwell. I could hear his heavy breathing.

"Mom, his mother is not there right now, but he said she'll be home a little after ten."

"Okay, then I'll talk to her a little after ten."

"Why?" He shouted. "Why can't I just leave and you talk to her when she gets home?"

"Because that's not how things work in this house."

"I hate this house and all these stupid rules," he exclaimed. "You always have to make a mountain out of a mole-hill. Other parent's don't take their children through all this crap. They don't worry about their children all the time. They give them freedom and let them have fun. When I grow up I'm never going to be the type of parent that sucks the fun out of everything."

"I'll talk to his mother when she gets home," I repeated.

"His mom is on her way home now," he pleaded.

"I'll talk to her when she gets home." I slowly stated with a little more clarity.

"The aunt is home and she's an adult."

"That's good, she's also hearing impaired, so I want to speak to the head of the house."

"Oh my God!" He screeched. "It's just a frickin' sleepover, what more do you want?" I could hear his rapid breathing over Darrin's snoring. "You want to control every frickin' thing. You think you know what's best for everybody, but you don't. You always want us stuck up in this stupid house. This is my life! I should be able to do what I want!"

I walked to the top of the stairs and looked down. He was looking up at me with rage and anger in his eyes.

"Son, you better go to your room quickly before I throw this Bible down there and knock some sense in your raggedy head. You are not going anywhere without me having confirmation of an adult's presence. If you don't like it that's your problem, not mine. You're welcome to get a high-paying job and move out and into your own apartment. These are the rules of this house and I'm not negotiating with a snot-nose, rude, obnoxious teenager."

"That's the problem, you make too many stupid frickin' rules." He shouted as he ran into his bedroom, slamming the door again. I could hear him grumbling profanities two floors up. I bowed my head and began praying.

During the night, I lightly dozed as I listened for the sound of doors and windows opening and closing. By sunrise Saturday morning, I was exhausted and extremely irritable, so when LaCrystal entered our bedroom and turned on the TV to a *Sponge-Bob Square-Pants* cartoon, I groaned. Placing the pillow over my face to block the sunlight and the loud irritating voice of the character, I rolled over to face the wall.

"Mommy," she whispered, softly shaking my foot, "Are you asleep?"

"No Sweetie, not anymore. Good morning."

"Morning Mommy," she said. "Last night, around two o'clock, three girls in flip-flops kept running up and down the sidewalk calling Quasim's name and knocking on his bedroom window. I peeked out my window and saw Quasim's friend leaning against the tree in our yard. And his friend's mother, she didn't come home until seven this morning. I heard her when she pulled into the parking lot and I peeked out my window and saw her get out the car and go into the house."

Now I understood why the feeling of dread was so overwhelming the previous night and why he was so irate at me for foiling their disastrous plans. I intended on approaching him, but I wanted to wait until the time was right.

All day Quasim avoided me. He cut his eyes, looked at me side-ways and left any room I entered. When dinner was over, I called him back to the dining room table.

"Son, which one of those little girls at the sleepover was supposed to be your partner for the night?"

"What are you talking about? What little girls?" He asked while turning his lip up and sneering at me in disgust.

"I'm talking about the arrangements that you and your friends made. Some girls woke LaCrystal up while they were trying to wake you last night."

He slowly pulled out a chair, sat at the table and quieted down. Busted.

"The girl that you were more than likely going to have sex with, because we both know that that was the objective, is she on contraceptives? Did you, who have *nooo* income, purchase condoms?" I asked, stretching the word 'no' to exaggerate it and make him aware of his financial state.

"No."

"What's her relationship like with her parents?"

"I don't know?"

"What does that little girl plan on doing after graduation?"

"I don't know all that. Nobody talks about that kind of stuff when they get together. Why are you always worrying about me anyway? This is my life!" He stated with a frown on his face.

"Because whatever you do, until you turn eighteen, it comes back on your parent's. So, your business is our business. And if the plans y'all supposedly made had taken a turn for the worse and she had become pregnant, what was she intending to do with the baby?"

"I don't know?"

"Seems like you don't know a lot of stuff today Quasim. Did you know that once your sperm is racing up her uterus like the Preakness, there are no second chances? Life is not like the Las Vegas slot machines. You can't pull the handle and get another chance.

"If you get anyone pregnant while you're living at home, I will insist that you get a job after school and take care of your child."

"But that's not your call, it's mine." He arrogantly stated.

"Not while you're a minor. If the teenage mother needs your social security number or a copy of your pay stub, I will give it to her." I stated as I expressionlessly looked at him.

He jumped up from the table, filled with rage and shouted, "You have no right to give anyone my personal information. That is wrong. That is where you cross the line."

"No son," I replied, using every ounce of self-control I could muster, "What is wrong is bringing a child into this world and not feeling like it's your responsibility to take care of it. Unless the female held you at gunpoint and demanded your sperm, you were a willing partner, and you're just as much responsible as her. It takes a real punk-ass to walk-away from his own child, and it ain't happening in this house as long as I have breath in my body."

"Well isn't that what welfare is for?" He sneered while casually leaning against the retaining wall.

My mouth went dry. I closed my eyes. I wanted to knock him clear into space.

"Father God, I know that You are real and I need for You to send a Word, a miracle, some understanding, or something—quick, because this boy is about to take me there, and I don't know if I can control myself," I whispered, "Lord I need you now."

I opened my eyes. Quasim was staring at me like I was just shy of a strait-jacket.

"Son, you better wake up or life is going to take you on a vicious spin cycle. Welfare is not the cure for anyone's stupidity or rebellious mistakes, and abortion is not a form of birth-control. If you choose to have unprotected sex, that is ultimately your choice, but as long as you live under my roof, you will take care of any child you conceive, willfully or by force. And yes, I will drive the young lady down to the courthouse myself to file child support papers against you. And if you still refuse to acknowledge your responsibilities, you will have to find somewhere else to live."

"Either way, it's still my choice," he snapped, "And just like my rap career, you don't support that. You don't know how far I could go in life if I had the chance. I might make it big as a rapper and become a star one day, but all you do is try to run my life and discourage my dreams, but I know what I want out of life."

"Quasim, I don't want to live your life or ruin your life," I said, "I'm trying to help you see the truth in reality. At sixteen, you think you have it all sorted out, but you don't. The choices and decisions you're making right now won't lead you to the glamorous life, but they will lead you to the poor-house and maybe the courthouse. Do you have any idea as to what kind of mother that girl would be to your child if you had had sex with her and she became pregnant? Would she be abusive? Would your child end up in foster-care?

"I don't know, I didn't think about that," he piped down, pondering the questions before honestly answering.

"Did you think of how many days you would have to miss from school because as a teenage father, you may have to go to court to gain custody of your child? Did you think of how much this might cost financially? Especially if the courts deemed you too young and unprepared to care for the child, did you ever think of the burden that would put on us if we had to chip-in and help raise your child?

"Well-well no," he stammered and looked down at his lap. "No one ever put it to me like that. It sounds different when you look at it from your perspective."

"Everything I am telling you is pure fact. I'm not sugar coating or deceiving you. I'm not jealous of your youth or your raging sex drive. Sex is a very powerful and over-rated physical pleasure that God gave us to enjoy with our marriage partner, but if we abuse it, we will pay a high price, one that most people aren't willing to pay. As my child, it is my duty to make sure you know, that as Jesus Christ is my Savior, you will not be allowed to walk-away from your responsibility and leave it as a burden for someone else as long as you live in my house."

"What if I left your house? What if I moved in with friends?"

"Please show me a friend or any family willing to take in a jobless, disrespectful, teenager with a bad attitude and a screaming infant, and I will send you off with my paycheck."

Darrin came downstairs, looked at Quasim with disgust, and shook his head from side-to-side.

"I have heard enough." He shouted. "Quasim whether you want to believe it or not, your mother is trying to correct your warped way of thinking because she loves you. You think your friends and the world are looking out for you and have your best interest at heart, but they don't. They'll use you up and spit you out like a watermelon seed. Your friends don't care where you'll end up in life and the world doesn't give a damn if you become another teenage father, go to prison, or get shot dead, we do. But right now you're so filled with pride, rebellion, stubbornness and raging hormones, you can't see that you're making your mother the enemy while honoring your foolish friends. You think you and your friends know everything—"

"I'm not saying I know everything, she—"

"She's doing the right thing. Period." Darrin interrupted. "Do you think your friends invented sneakiness and sex? Do they know how to teach you how to make it in this world? My God, this is ridiculous." He shouted, throwing his hands up in the air. "Kelley, that's it. Come upstairs now. This conversation is over."

I followed him up the stairs. After showering, we got into bed, snuggled and watched rerun episodes of *Seinfeld*.

Later that night, Quasim came upstairs to our bedroom and apologized. He thanked us for intervening in his life and we thanked him for acknowledging our parental guidance. I added another silent prayer for him to the numerous ones already stacked up.

Chapter 35

Earthquake

I sat up in bed and listened. Had I heard something or was I dreaming? It was a beautiful, sunny Friday afternoon in June, my fortieth birthday and I was bedridden and heavily medicated on Vicodin, hoping to ease my ongoing severe lower back-pain. Silence. I waited a few seconds before closing my eyes and lying back—BOOM! BOOM! BOOM!

My eyes sprang open and I slowly sat up. Carefully making my way down the stairs to the front door, I was met in the dining room by LaCrystal and Travonté, who had been in the basement watching TV. They came running up to me screaming with their hands flailing. Reaching out to me, LaCrystal slammed her body into mine and grabbed me tightly around the waist. Burying her face in my neck, she screamed uncontrollably.

Before I could fully grasp what was happening, I heard a deafening thud. The front door swung open with massive force, slamming into the wall before shifting off its hinges, leaving a large hole where the knob made contact. A SWAT Team dressed in all black from head-to-toe stormed into our home aiming loaded laser-sighted rifles at us. Travonté crouched behind me, using my body as a human shield.

"Quake! Quake!" I heard the SWAT Team shouting in the mass of confusion.

Through my children's chaotic screaming and pulling on my clothes and under the influence of the Vicodin, my brain and reflexes refused to cooperate.

"What is an earthquake? Who's having an earthquake? We don't have earthquakes on the East Coast." I heard myself saying. Travonté was calling out to me and LaCrystal was still clinging to my shirt with her eyes squeezed tightly shut.

I watched, mesmerized by the tactically planned organization of the operation and wondered if this were a surreal dream. Members of the SWAT Team ran past us, casting us aside with their huge, heavily equipped bodies. Some ran up the stairs, while others in pairs, at the response to hand movements separated and headed for the basement. They were fast, organized and proficient.

I could hear doors opening and slamming shut above and beneath us. It was as if I were watching a slow-moving dream unfolding before my eyes. I looked out into the back yard and saw more members of the SWAT Team appearing. They moved quickly and quietly up the deck stairs, slid open the glass door, and ran past us. I clung to my children as tightly as they clung to me; for safety, for life.

Travonté and LaCrystal's screams echoed in my ears as they pleaded for me to protect them. Standing in the foyer, I felt completely helpless. My ears and eyes could hear and see everything, but my brain refused to process and react to the situation.

Shower curtains in the bathroom above our heads were snatched open and ripped from the metal rods, furniture was being turned over and mattresses were slammed down onto box-springs as the SWAT Team went from room to room, stopping briefly to yell, "Clear!"

I turned and looked out the front door and saw a massive man coming up the porch steps. He ducked as he crossed the threshold, and entered where the front door had been only seconds ago. His eyes made contact with mine. He was a behemoth of a man, the biggest and tallest I had ever seen. He could have easily been a Caucasian match to John Coffey in the movie, *The Green Mile*. He wore a brown Rappahannock, Virginia, Captain's uniform that bulged at the buttons, revealing slits of his stark white t-shirt underneath as he took his position in our foyer.

Flashing a piece of paper in my face, he quickly stuck it back into his shirt pocket before I could grab it and read it. He introduced himself as the captain. If he stated his name, my brain was so confused I would not have remembered it anyway.

"Am I being punked?" I heard myself ask out loud, craning my neck to look out the front door for that cute, brown-haired, guy that played on the TV sitcom, *The 70's Show* and produced the MTV *Punked* show.

As my eyes were drawn to the red dots pointed on my children's hearts and foreheads, they continued stepping on my toes in futile attempts to avoid the laser sights on the rifles. In my dense medicated state, their frantic screams sounded as if they were submerged in a pool of water. Somehow, those red-dots perked up my awareness just enough to comprehend that this was not a dream. Looking from the rifles and then back to my children, I closed my eyes and began to silently pray:

"God of Abraham, Maker of the heavens and the earth, I know that You are real. Please help me protect my children. Please clear the medications out of my system and allow me to focus on what is happening."

Opening my eyes, I watched the lips of the captain standing in the foyer repeating, "Quake-sim? Quake-sim?"

It clicked. "Oh, you're looking for Quasim?" I sluggishly asked.

"Yes Ma'am," the captain replied in a strong southern accent. "Do you know whar' your son Quake-sim is?"

"No, I don't."

Two more members of the SWAT Team appeared from the basement, brushed past us and headed up the stairs. Three others entered through the deck door and stood beside the captain. The initial pair continued standing at attention in front of us, as we meshed our bodies together like sleeping puppies. I counted a total of five holding their rifles aimed and ready at point blank range on us. I had no idea what Quasim was mixed-up in, but I was not about to suffer or allow my innocent children to suffer through this type of traumatic event any longer.

"Ma'am are you sure?"

I could feel my mind rapidly clearing and my anger swelled.

"Thank you Lord," I whispered. "Sure I'm sure. He works up the street at Taco Bell. Go and see if he's there."

"Ma'am do you know that harborin' a fugitive is against—"

"What?" I snapped, interrupting him and not caring one bit. "I don't uphold my children if they break the law. If they do something wrong, they're held accountable for their actions—and furthermore, why are you looking for him anyway?" I demanded with my hands, now balled into fists on my hips.

"Ma'am," he said, "As I stated earlier, we have a warrant for your son's arrest for gang related activity, gun and weapons charges, and a gang fight."

"Let me see the warrant." I challenged through clenched teeth. Turning to the SWAT Team, looking past their face masks, and directly into their eyes, I quietly stated: "This is my only daughter and if one your guns slip and you shoot her or any of my children, your entire force will have hell to pay. So unless you have some prophetic powers to raise the dead, I would advise you to get those damn red dots off my children because I will not accept, 'Oops, it was an accident.' God will have his revenge on Judgment Day, but I'll get mine now."

"Ma'am, ma'am—" the captain said, placing a hand in the air in an attempt to quiet me.

"And don't you have a picture of Quasim," I snapped at the captain, while jerking my neck back and forth and moving my head sharply from left to right in a 'sassy' motion. "Just to know what he looks like? Why would you come charging in my house without a clue as to who you're looking for? Why are you putting my other children in danger?"

"Ma'am, Ma'am—"

"No! Don't Ma'am me. My daughter is a female, with auburn hair for Christ's sake! And look at my son," I said, turning and pointing a finger at Travonté. "He has thick, curly black hair. There is no way you can say you thought either of them was Quasim. Do you even know who you're looking for, or did you just drive around assuming all black teenagers fit the description of Quasim?"

"Ma-am—"

"No. Don't feed me that bull. You knew Quasim's identity before you left the station—and take those damn rifles off of my children!" I shouted loudly. "If Quasim did something wrong, then you make him pay, but when you have rifles aimed at innocent children, I have a problem with that."

I walked over to the captain standing in the corner of the foyer slowly with my children right next to me, and looking up into his eyes, because at this point I was willing to protect my children with my life, or death if necessary, I said, "A life for a life."

"Ma'am, there is no need to get upset—are you threatening me?" The captain abruptly asked in the middle of his sentence. He took a step towards me.

"A life for a life." I repeated as I reached behind me without turning around and pulled Travonté and LaCrystal's bodies closer to mine to protect them.

The captain stared at me for a few seconds then looked at his team and without speaking, motioned to them to lower their weapons.

"I will personally bring Quasim to your department as soon as he walks through the door, this I promise. And why can't I see that warrant?"

"Ma'am you can go down to the courthouse and get a copy of the warrant."

"Why can't I see the one in your hand, isn't it the same as the one on file?"

"Ma'am, this one has other defendants' names on it and because they're minors, I'm not allowed to let you view it."

As he spoke, he raised his left hand and the SWAT Team slowly retreated out the front door. The captain descended the stairs after them, but turned to me as he reached the bottom step and said, "Ma'am, we'll go to his job. We're sorry for any inconvenience we have caused."

Like a tornado, they were gone as quickly as they had come, leaving behind weeping and destruction. Had LaCrystal and Travonté not been visibly shaken, distraught and clinging to me, I would have probably thought it was a nightmare.

All I could do was pray as uncontrollable emotions overwhelmed me and tears streamed down my face. I still had no clue as to why my home was raided. I was angry as hell, humiliated and confused and I wanted to hit something, Quasim, a wall, anything to release this frustration. Instead I wept.

Being thankful that Quasim was not home, because things would have taken a nasty turn, I pulled my cell phone out of my pocket and called Darrin, who was at work, and tried to relay the chain of events.

A few hours later he came home. He inspected and repaired the minor damage to the front door as I sat on a kitchen stool calling Quasim's cell phone. Receiving no answer, I began going through my phone listing and called all of his friends.

Darrin left to go back to work, but told me to call if I needed him. I waved him off and went back to concentrating on the phone calls. One mother answered her phone seconds before the SWAT Team burst into her home. The muscles in my neck tightened as I listened to her helpless, hysterical screams. She dropped the phone, but I could hear loud shouting and screaming in the background. My hands were trembling as I hung up.

Friends quickly relayed messages to Quasim and he rushed home immediately. As he came through the front door, I could see his lips rapidly moving, but I was so filled with rage, it all sounded foreign. After telling him the details of the police raiding my home in search of him, I told him to shower and put on extra underwear, because where I was taking him, I was sure he would not be returning home with me.

Gathering my children, I drove Quasim to the local precinct. At the station we were met by a female officer, who questioned Quasim briefly. He was handcuffed and led away laughing and singing rap songs; either out of defiance, humiliation, or sheer stupidity, I'm not sure which. The officer told me where and when to appear for his arraignment, which was the following Monday morning.

It was out of our hands now. I knew I had to step back and allow the Lord to break and change my son. This was going to be a very difficult and painful journey for all of us, but I knew that I had to avoid becoming a helicopter Mom and obstruct the law in my son's defense. I had a knack for over-protecting, but this time he had to learn from his own mistakes.

We drove home in silence. Since no one felt like eating, we skipped dinner and went to bed early. But throughout the night, I heard doors opening and closing, and knew, like myself, none of us got much sleep.

At 8:30 Monday morning we walked into a packed, standing-room only Juvenile Relations Courthouse waiting area. Nearly an hour later, we were able to squeeze onto the hard wooden benches, knee-to-knee with other families, like sardines in a can, as we waited for our sons name to be called.

I quietly scanned the room of various faces and colors. The common bond was the defeat and fear on each of our faces. Parent's bouncing cranky toddlers on their laps looked around uneasily. Teenagers nervously laughed as they attempted to make small talk with relatives. No one dared to speak of their problem or befriend anyone else. Everyone was a possible witness.

I felt like our children were part of a seemingly lost and misguided generation, stumbling around in a haze of rebellious darkness, creating a blanket of broken, angry, parents, caregivers and relatives. I squeezed Darrin's hand. We too, were interwoven into that blanket.

Six hours later, Quasim's name was called. Entering the courtroom, we were quickly redirected off to the side and into a small closet-sized office. An over-sized desk sat in the middle of the room, taking up much of the space. The door was closed behind us by a broad shouldered man with sandy hair, pale blue eyes and a prominent chin. He introduced himself as Quasim's court-appointed attorney.

He asked us a barrage of questions about our son as he rapidly jotted notes. We listened as Quasim's name was called over the intercom system three minutes later. A female officer opened the door, stuck her head into the little room and demanded we follow her.

Taking designated seats in the first row behind the attorney, we watched as a very young judge shuffled and read documents placed in front of him. As the blur of judicial jargon between attorneys, prosecutors, probation officers and the judge, over indictment charges, witnesses and the upcoming hearing date, like a school-girl, I raised my hand to ask a question. A bailiff quickly came toward me and told me to put my hand down, there would be no questions asked. Scorned and angry, I sat still and patiently waited for all of it to be over.

As parents, we had no rights, power or voice. Everything was left up to the courts. Craning my neck, I was able to see my son on the large monitor that hung from the ceiling, adjacent to the judge's desk. I gasped as he answered 'yes' and 'no' questions presented to him by the judge. Dark ringlets encircled his blood-shot swollen eyes, validating that he had been crying for an extended period of time. My heart ached for him. His haggard expression and unkempt hair made me feel absolutely helpless as a parent. I rested my head on Darrin's shoulder and cried, wiping my nose and eyes with my sleeve.

Sitting up when the same young blond officer, who a few years earlier, had begged me not to prosecute two elementary and middle school aged neighborhood terrors after they shot Desmond in the face with a pellet gun, he introduced himself not as an officer anymore, but as Detective Crawford.

Turning to whisper and possibly jog Darrin's memory, I was immediately hushed again by the bailiff standing guard. I was furious.

Detective Crawford addressed the court and told them of the Gang-Drug Terrorism Unit that was set-up to break passwords and monitor activity on social networks such as; MySpace and Face book. He presented enough online gang affiliation and evidence to indict several middle and high school students.

We were told that our son and approximately fifteen other students were initiated through social network sites into the MOB (Money over Bitches) and the Bloods gang. As their online verbal disputes escalated into a gang fight, it was all that the police needed to proceed with arrests. Even though no guns or knives were used in the fights, found on the premises, or found on the kids, just rocks, sticks, sand and fists, charges were put on their records that would affect them for a lifetime.

Darrin and I were asked to stand and leave the courtroom. We were ushered out by the bailiff, but told not to leave until we received our son's paperwork. I quickly stole a glance back and saw another frightened teenager sit down in the exact chair Quasim previously sat in. His eyes anxiously scanned the courtroom in search of his family members.

Letting the heavy oak door slowly close behind me, I took Darrin's arm as he led me back to the hard benches. Bleak, weary faces nervously watched us as we found a spot for two. Darrin tried, to the best of his ability, to whisper and explain the court proceedings to me.

A short while later Quasim's court appointed attorney exited the courtroom. I watched as his eyes searched faces until he found ours. He motioned for us to meet him in the main hall. In an additional five minutes, he ran through the court proceedings, told us to keep waiting for our son's documents, explained to us where we could inquire about visitations and his missed homework assignments. He handed us his business card, wished us luck, and rushed back into the waiting area calling out the next teenager's name he would be representing so he could meet the parents a few minutes before they went before the judge.

Over the next few weeks of court appearances, hearings, and visitations, Darrin and I were able to confront Detective Crawford and question his ethical practices. As for the arrested students, they began breaking friendships and telling on each other. Within a three month period, all of the juvenile students involved were pressured into pleading guilty to all pending charges, even the charges where there was no evidence and that were completely false. They were scared so some of them took guilty pleas in their desperation to be quickly released.

This traumatic ordeal took my family through emotional and physical hell. Quasim learned many lessons in how his behavior affected his life. He saw first-hand that when you are on the wrong side of the judicial system; friends betray you, and you have absolutely no rights behind bars. Your education is compromised and what you thought was making you popular, liked by everyone and cool, really broke trust and credibility with people who really did love you.

Even when Quasim did not know it, Darrin and I were praying for him and all of our children. We knew that they had the potential to do great things and go far in life, but we also knew that "they" had to believe this for themselves. We prayed they were not permanently tripped up by life's temptations, obstacles, and set-backs.

LaCrystal had been accepted through an (EAP) Early Acceptance Program to attend Hampton University in Hampton, Virginia the upcoming fall. She was looking forward to graduating, leaving home, living on campus and pursuing college life. She saw that many of her graduating classmates did not make it to college and she was extremely appreciative that she had listened to her parents; made good grades, stayed out of trouble with the law, stayed out of trouble with the opposite sex, and wanted more out of life then the 20 hours a week issued to its workers in the local restaurants.

We were praying Quasim, Travonté and Desmond realized that the dream of college could be obtained for them too. We hoped they would all be encouraged to set goals and push themselves. As parents, we could only do so much, the leg work rested on the child's shoulders.

When he returned home, Quasim choose to hang out with one or two close friends and kept out of trouble. In his spare time he worked and made rap CD's with his friends. I saw the changes in his behavior. I saw how he avoided people that he knew were on the express train to nowhere city. Former friends that used to hang-out on the front porch were no longer seen. He went to school, did his homework (without a hassle), and worked a part-time job.

Readers, for a few years he became a model student. He cleaned up after himself, his side of the room stayed neat and tidy. He respected us and his brother's personal space. And listen to this, no teachers, principals, or school officials called to report any type of rudeness, disrespect or actions that would lead to a suspension all the way up to his graduation date.

Chapter 36
A Political View

"Ma, can I vote this year?" Quasim asked while biting into a crunchy fried chicken drumstick .

From the kitchen, I peered at him through the breakfast-bar opening as I fixed my dinner plate. "Oh, how I have waited to hear those words escape your lips."

"What the heck does that mean?" He asked through a mouthful, furrowing his eyebrows and turning the corner of his lip up at me.

Coming into the dining room, I sat my plate down on the placemat, said grace, and began eating.

"Anyway," he continued, "Have you been following that man named Obama?"

"Yes, I have."

"Well, what do you think of him?" He asked scooping up a spoonful of baked beans and shoveling them into his mouth.

I sat at the dinner table; Desmond to my right, Quasim to my left and Travonté at the opposite end. They continued quietly eating. Darrin decided not to eat dinner and had gone to bed early.

"I think Mr. Obama's life, marriage, family history and career are not coincidences. I believe God has a plan for him just like he had for Moses and Joseph."

"But do you think that is enough for him to become president?"

I took a drink of tea, swallowed and stated with assurance,

"Son, he will become America's first African-American President."

"I don't think so," Quasim replied. "There is too much deep hatred towards blacks in America."

"That's why his makeup is so unique." I said as I picked up a spoonful of mashed potatoes, "Obama has the blood of many nations flowing through his veins."

"That still won't stop some racist idiot from attempting to harm him."

"No racist idiot can stand against God's plan." I replied covering my mouth with my hand as I chewed.

"Ma, he has a Muslim name and even though he's extremely intelligent, they say he may not even be from Amer—"

"Quasim," I interrupted, turning and looking to my left, directly at him, "Keep your doubt to yourself. Doubt is fear and blacks have been doubtful and fearful for far too long. As long as there are humans on earth, we'll have haters and jealousy. I believe the dream will be fulfilled in this man. He will be the 44th President of the United States."

"Well I don't think so." Quasim mumbled under his breath.

Travonté and Desmond continued listening, glancing up every so often, and eating in silence.

"What about Hilary Clinton?" Quasim blurted out.

"She would make an excellent presidential candidate. She has knowledge, experience and is committed to the American people. Either of them would make an honorable president, and anyway, it's time for a change."

After everyone finished dinner, we continued sitting at the table talking.

"Once I'm eighteen, I can vote for whoever I choose, can't I?" Quasim asked.

"Yes son, but your fight as a juvenile may be your biggest obstacle."

"But that's over and done. I paid my debt to society."

Quasim stated in a higher than normal tone.

Sliding my plate away from me, I leaned back and relaxed my head on the back of the parson chair. "Unfortunately, lawmakers in the states of Virginia and Kentucky don't feel the same way. They may not believe a person can change or should be given forgiveness after making a mistake. So they made laws to permanently disenfranchise anyone with run-ins with the law, regardless if they were a juvenile or not, and stop them from having voting rights. I believe that ludicrous law is for as long as they live."

"That's absolutely ridiculous. Who thinks up this kind of crap to turn it into a law? I'm going to find out how I can legally fight that." Quasim snapped, sucking his teeth.

"Are you and Dad voting?" Desmond softly asked.

"Yes."

"Did you vote in the primaries?" Desmond inquired.

"Yes," I calmly replied, turning to my right and looking at him with interest. "Only death or imprisonment would have stopped us."

This was the first time any of our children showed any interest in politics (except when it was bath time and Desmond decided to scream about his inalienable rights in a democratic society), and I was elated. This presidential election was the topic of conversations everywhere. When it took precedence in our home over football, girls, food and sibling bickering, I was willing to answer all questions.

Quasim was becoming visibly frustrated. Even though I understood how unfair it was, and it did seem like he was being sentenced twice, I wanted to help him see that these medieval laws that were put into place were also part of his consequences for his actions. I wanted each of them to learn the overall lesson of how criminal charges affect the individual's life long after the incident is over.

"Mom," Desmond asked, "Are you and Dad democrat,

republican or independent?"

"We're Democrat."

"Why?" He inquired. "What made you choose Democrat over the others?"

"For five years, I was a single mother and for fifteen months I relied on government assistance. I received welfare, food stamps, Medicaid and WIC. Contrary to liberal or public opinion, everyone on welfare is not sitting home waiting on a fat $300.00 monthly check to buy beer and drugs. I've always despised drinking and drugs. My child support enforcement case had not been enforced at the time, and it became impossible for me to keep a full-time job and care for a sick infant. The first two years of LaCrystal's life, she was in and out Children's Hospital so often I had to leave my job. I lost my apartment and ended up homeless. I was eventually placed in the Pitts Homeless Shelter in Washington, DC. It was there that I found out about job training programs offered to low-income mothers on welfare."

I noticed no one got up to refill glasses of tea, scrape pots, or interrupted me. I had their attention so I sat up and kept talking.

"The programs were set into place when President Jimmy Carter, a democrat, was in office. The one I enrolled in was called ARC (A Real Chance)."

"Is the ARC program still in existence?" Desmond inquired, placing his elbows on the table and looking at me with interest.

"No baby, as soon as the president after him, who I believe was Ronald Reagan, a republican, came into office, they cut all funding to programs that helped the people get on their feet and focused on funding Desert Storm.

"That program paid for 90% of daycare expenses while I attended Strayer College (which they paid for also), where I was taught job preparedness, entry level computer training, interview skills, and sent on interviews. I would not have the federal government job that I have today, and I've been on the same job for nearly twenty-five years, if it had not been for that program."

"So because the democrats provided opportunities for you, you're faithful to their party?" Desmond asked.

"I'm faithful to any party that empowers the people instead of labeling them. Any party that opens doors to financial independence and if the Democratic Party addresses issues that relates to the common American, I'm onboard."

"Oh." He responded.

Quasim who had been muddled and silent for a while, took his fork, scraped it across his plate, then blurted out, "So you don't think Barack Obama's being black will influence you?"

How did I know? How did I know he would ask the tactless questions?

He looked at me with raised eyebrows, anticipating the answer.

"I am proud of the fact that he is an intelligent, committed, family oriented, black man. I think he will be an excellent example to millions of minorities. The fact that he doesn't have a criminal record and was confident enough to set goals and go after them means a lot to me. So yes, I am proud to honor him as a black man. But I'm voting for him because of his political background and his commitment to the American people."

"What about McCain?" Quasim asked with indifference.

"What about him?"

"How do you feel about all that stuff Bill Clinton did when he was President? Do you think it will affect his wife if she runs for President?" Quasim blurted, changing the subject.

"Hilary is her own woman. With or without her husband she is strong and committed to do whatever is necessary to rebuild America."

"I'm making good decisions with my life too and I'm going to college and I'm going to major in engineering." Desmond added with a broad smile.

"Kiss up." Quasim snarled.

"No I'm not." Desmond retaliated.

"Quasim, leave him alone. He has a dream and a focus. You get your act together and don't worry about him. Like the old folks say, "Clean out your own backyard before you go cleaning out someone else's backyard." Furthermore, it's getting late," I said as I got up to go into the kitchen and answer the ringing phone. "Let's clear the table and get ready for bed, ya'll have school tomorrow."

It was LaCrystal calling from college. She too was excited about the elections and was working on one of the campaigns at her college. The school took the students by bus loads to neighboring communities and they went door-to-door signing up people to vote. She said it made her feel like she was back in the 60's and she was so happy to be a part of such a monumental and historical experience she started to cry. She told me that the school took the students by bus loads to Richmond to see the Presidential elect Barak Obama speak and she was able to hear him up close and personal.

Meanwhile, the boys washed dishes and cleaned the kitchen before going to bed. After hanging up with LaCrystal, I was so happy I went up the stairs to our room singing and smiling.

Chapter 37
Shopping Cart Lifting

I had a strong craving for hot, chewy, homemade chocolate chip cookies one spring Saturday afternoon so I skipped downstairs to the kitchen and began preparing the batter. Halfway through blending the mixture, I realized there were no eggs. Choosing not to waste gas by driving a mere four blocks to the local Food Lion grocery store, I bundled and twisted my hair up in a colorful scarf and tied a knot in the center of my forehead. Throwing on oversized sweat pants, a large ratty shirt that hung down to my knees, and comfortable floppy croc shoes, I looked at myself in the mirror. I definitely wouldn't win any fashion awards. Putting my cell phone on the charger, I grabbed my keys and my wallet on the way out the front door. I was only going to purchase eggs, no problem.

My total was $64.10. Plastic bags filled with canned vegetables, tuna, pork & beans, frozen meats, bread, cereal, and anything else on sale or on the clearance aisle were all squeezed onto the cart and purchased at the register.

Walking to the parking lot, I felt around in my pockets for my car keys as I scanned the area. Stopping and turning in circles, I pushed the panic button in hopes of hearing the alarm. Silence. I pushed the button again to make my car alarm go off and listened intently. Nothing. *If someone stole my—Crap! I didn't drive my car.* I began frantically patting my pockets in search of my cell phone so I could call Darrin and ask him to come pick me up. Crap! Crap!! Crap!!! The phone was home on the charger. My only solutions were to take all of the food back (excluding the eggs), or push the cart containing my groceries home.

Just the thought of tasting delicious, warm chocolate chip cookies sealed my decision. Rearranging all of the breakable and fragile groceries, I placed the bread and eggs on top, boxed items in the middle, and moved canned goods to the front. I proceeded deeper into the mass of cars. Out of the corner of my eye, I could see a young man collecting shopping carts. He waited patiently to add mine to the line he was already pushing.

Walking slowly through cars, I made a quick U–turn, and headed out of the parking lot. Running around the corner, the large metal cart wobbled and clanked loudly up the hill as I forced it to go faster. It was hot and humid and the weight of the groceries combined with the heat and my baggy clothes caused me to sweat and nearly collapse from exhaustion. I blinked away the little stars that danced in front of my eyes but kept running, cursing myself for not buying a bottle of water when I was in the store.

The loaf of bread fell off the cart. Reaching down and picking it up in one swoop, I threw it back on top and glanced behind me. The young man had followed me to the corner and was scratching and shaking his head and looking at me with a puzzled expression.

The asphalt connecting with the metal wheels made loud clacking and rattling sounds. One broken front right wheel kept spinning wildly, forcing the cart off in the opposite direction.

"I'll bring it back!" I yelled back at him.

He may have mistaken me for a crazy lady, but appearances were my least concern, I needed to get my groceries home without him calling the police for shopping cart-lifting.

I made it to the top of the hill and stopped to catch my breath. Standing on the side of the road, I lifted the corners of my shirt to wipe the sweat from my face. I noticed the street was becoming a lot more gravelly, so, I grabbed the handle tightly and kept forcefully pushing in the pursuit of home. Rolling over the pebbles and rocks made an even louder deafening clatter and caused the cart to shake unsteadily.

Cars whizzed past. People slowed down and craned their necks to gawk at me, like they never saw a sweaty, black lady with a raggedy scarf wrapped around her head, pushing a rattling cart filled with groceries down the street before. I stuck my tongue out at a few nosey rubber-neckers and rolled my eyes at others.

Entering my neighborhood, I hit a bump and that same stupid loaf of bread fell and landed on the yellow painted asphalt. As I bent to pick it up, two cans of pork & beans tumbled out of the cart and rolled down the street towards the sewer. After retrieving the bread, I chased the runaway pork & beans and placed them in the cart.

Travonté was sitting on the top porch step eating and spitting sunflower seeds into the bushes when he spotted me coming down the hill. He stood up, threw his hands in the air in a, who-knows gesture then mouthed, "What the—?"

Getting closer, I went over another yellow speed bump and a can of green beans fell to the street and rolled away.

"Instead of standing there staring at me like I'm crazy, you need to come here and pick up your dinner." I yelled.

Quasim, whom I had not seen, was also sitting on the porch listening to his iPod. He stood up, took the plugs out of his ears and looked around. He shook his head.

"This is so embarrassing." Travonté shouted, shaking his head from side-to-side as he briskly jog-walked towards me. "This is the most humiliating thing you have ever done. You look like a homeless lady. This is ridiculous."

"Pick up the green beans Travonté and shut your trap. It's too hot out here to be fussing with you."

He walked over, snatched the green beans up as it rolled

towards him, and slammed the can onto the cart. Rolling his eyes in annoyance, he turned and ran to the house.

Quasim leaned on the porch rail and watched me in disbelief before turning and quickly running into the house. I grabbed the eggs off the top and allowed the cart to roll the last few feet and bang into the curb. Both boys were standing in the kitchen peering out of the mini-blinds whispering loudly about me.

"Do I look like I care what you two ingrates think about me? Ya'll better come out here and get these groceries, or you won't eat." I said as I climbed the steps, holding tightly to the black wrought iron railing. "And ya'll better get all of those damn sunflower-seeds off of my porch and out of my bushes."

"You are the most embarrassing mother in the world." Travonté groaned as he opened the front door and walked out. "You are absolutely freakin' ridiculous."

"No, she's crazy," Quasim concluded as he followed Travonté outside. "She needs therapy."

After they grudgingly carried the groceries into the house and placed the bags on the kitchen floor, they turned to go outside again. I listened as they complained about my appearance and my inexcusable behavior.

"Excuse me son," I said to Travonté as I opened the carton and counted three broken eggs. "I need for you to push that cart back to the grocery store before they send the police out looking for me."

Travonté's mouth dropped open and his dark eyes bulged like a hoot owl in the night as he looked at me in horror.

"What do you mean? Do you expect me to push that cart back up to the store? I have a reputation to uphold. There could be girls up there. I can't be seen pushing grocery carts. What are you trying to do, damage my credibility? I'm not old and crazy like you."

"Son, I promise, no one is thinking about you, and anyway, I didn't see any pretty girls in the store."

"Please, I beg of you, this isn't right. This could damage a kid for life," he pleaded.

"Travonté, please take the cart back and stop being so dramatic. Geez."

"Please, I could be emotionally scarred. I'll need therapy for life."

"Son, make sure the young man collecting the carts sees you. He will know who took the cart."

"What!" He shrieked, "Someone saw you take the cart?"

He closed his eyes, tilted his head towards the ceiling and groaned loudly. "Oh God, this can't be happening. You live to punish us with embarrassment. You want us to have heart attacks and die at an early age."

"Travonté, take the cart back and stop carrying on."

"This is the most outrageous thing you've ever done. This just takes the—and then you get me involved in your schemes." He complained as he walked outside, got the cart, and ran clattering up the sidewalk.

It seemed like everything I did caused them some type of embarrassment. I was beginning to enjoy the advantages of getting older.

Epilogue

LaCrystal

After attending Hampton University and transferring to Old Dominion University she earned a Bachelor's Degree in English. She pursued graduate studies in Fashion Design at The San Francisco Academy of Art and Design before joining the United States Army.

LaCrystal grew into a beautiful, self-reliant and confident young woman. She is paving her own way in life and we are proud of her and happy for her. We pray for God's protection all around her as she accomplishes her dreams.

Quasim

Years of confrontations, disrespect and refusing to adhere to family rules, took its toll on my health. A few months after turning eighteen and yet another heated argument, Quasim was told to leave the home.

He moved in with friends and even though we stayed in touch and supported his new independence, we knew we could no longer find peace while living together. After graduating from high school, I assisted him in finding a job and enrolling in Garrett College and Germanna Community College. He was accepted to both colleges, but later chose to attend Northern Virginia Community College.

He remains independent and self-reliant. We pray for God's protection and guidance over him as Quasim finds his way in the world. We believe all of his short-comings are molding him to become a powerful man of God. In the meantime, as he continues to mature and grow, we keep him in prayer.

Travonté

Peer influences and the use of marijuana may have contributed to Travonté becoming defiant and disrespectful, or it could have been just plain old teenage rebellion. Therapy was shunned and verbal warnings fell on deaf ears. His loss of focus made a major impact on academics during his senior year and affected graduation.

A few weeks before his nineteenth birthday, the drug use took its toll and after an explosive confrontation, he too was asked to leave the home. He moved in with family members, began working various jobs, and within a year or two, he was in trouble with the law.

We encourage him whenever we can and keep him lifted up in prayer. He has given his life to the Lord and now seeks spiritual guidance on a daily basis. We know that God can use anyone and every situation for good, so we look forward to seeing where He leads Travonté.

Desmond

After a childhood of running from his brothers and the state police, Desmond began running for recognition. He won numerous ribbons, awards, trophies, and State and District Titles in Track and Field events in high school.

He excelled in a college preparatory, honors, Dual Enrollment, and Advanced Placement (AP) curriculums. He received scholarships to several colleges and with the help of an excellent track coach, signed a letter of intent to attend Virginia Military Institute (VMI) to study Engineering. We continue to lift him up in prayer and look forward to seeing him succeed in life as he pursues the path God has placed him on.

Darrin and Kelley

I could say life is sweet and all of the problems were over after the children left home. I could even say we lived some 'Lollipop-Gumdrop' happily ever-after fairy tale, but that would be a lie and this book is about being honest and real.

The highly stressful situations left a terrible void and nearly ripped our marriage apart. Somehow, we lost our focus and let our guards down. The enemy slipped in, attacked, and almost conquered. Outside influences took priority over our marriage commitment and we forgot our sole purpose for coming together as husband and wife.

After falling deeply into sin, God stepped in. Not only did Darrin give his life to Christ, I rededicated my life to the Lord too.

Through prayer, forgiveness, therapy and accountability to each other, we are trying to salvage our marriage in God's presence. We pray that as a couple we can walk by faith and not by sight and live by the spirit and not by the flesh.

I deeply thank you for reading my first book. I hope you enjoyed the journey and I pray you have found something that may help you with your teenagers.

God bless

Author S. Kelley Chambers
Learn more about Kelley and her book by visiting:
www.skchambers.com

CPSIA information can be obtained
at www.ICGtesting.com
Printed in the USA
FSHW02n2041090918
51983FS